P9-EDK-532

A Flame In Barbed Wire

A Flame In Barbed Wire

The Story of Amnesty International

Egon Larsen

W · W · NORTON & COMPANY
New York

Library of Congress Cataloging in Publication Data
Larsen, Egon, 1904-
    A flame in barbed wire.

    Includes index.
    1. Amnesty International—History.   I. Title.

HV7240.L44   1979   365'.45'0621   79-11676
ISBN 0-393-01213-1

1 2 3 4 5 6 7 8 9 0

Contents

List of Illustrations

Foreword

Amnesty International is an organization with little opportunity to look backward, to take the time to tell its own history. Continually faced with crises and changing situations—incarceration of a group of people, usually prisoners of conscience, in one country, reports of prisoners being tortured in another, an appeal against an impending execution in yet another—there is little chance for its volunteer members or its staff to tell the story of Amnesty's seventeen years of existence. Also, because Amnesty International has made the prudent decision not to claim credit for the release of prisoners whose cases it has taken up, it dislikes elaborate publicity. But most importantly, the specific human rights problems on which Amnesty International works are not disappearing from the world and may even be increasing. This leads its members to be always looking ahead rather than contemplating past successes and failures in their work of seeking the release of men and women detained anywhere for their beliefs, color, sex, ethnic origin, language, or religion, providing they have neither used nor advocated violence; advocating fair and early trials for all political prisoners; and opposing the death penalty and torture of all prisoners, without reservation.

Egon Larsen has performed the most useful function of telling the history of Amnesty International in a lively and accessible way. He begins by describing the modest, tentative beginnings of the movement with Peter Benenson's now famous article in the *Observer* on the "forgotten prisoners," and the extraordinary worldwide reaction of support and approval. He then traces the first years of Amnesty International as it established itself as a truly international organization and struggled to win recognition for its concerns. He gives case histories—always the central focus of Amnesty's work—and describes the evolution within the organization of growing concern with the institutionalization of torture and the use of the death penalty. He describes some of the problems and debates within Amnesty and the issues behind them. Considering that Mr. Larsen had no special access to Amnesty International's files and was not writing an authorized history of the organization, he has done a most credible and skillfull job of describing its history. An official Amnesty International publication is written in a style which bends over backward to be measured, fair, and unemotional in its presentation, whereas Mr. Larsen, writing for the general public, has the advantage of being able to give his readers a lively and popular account of Amnesty International's work and history. A *Flame in Barbed Wire* is certain to be a useful book for those interested in Amnesty International and, especially, for new members of the organization.

—A. Whitney Ellsworth
Member, Board of Directors
Amnesty International USA

A Flame In Barbed Wire

1

Birth and Youth of a Movement

A Toast to Freedom

A great thaw in international affairs seemed to have set in and mankind was sighing with relief. The 'cold war', which had begun almost as soon as the second World War ended, looked like fizzling out. The year was 1960; the Korean war was long over and as good as forgotten, the Suez adventure was also sinking into well-deserved oblivion, and Hungary was slowly recovering from the trauma of the Russian invasion. In the United States, the hysterical fear of Communism which had spawned the House Committee on 'Un-American Activities' was on the wane now that its Chairman McCarthy was dead and gone — politically and physically. A British Prime Minister had visited Moscow for the first time, and the Pope had received his first Communist visitor — the Soviet leader Khrushchev who, compared to his predecessor Stalin, seemed to be much more of a human being, last but not least because of his sense of humour.

I was in Russia on a students' package tour early in that year, curious to find out how the country was shaping after the Stalin era. People dared to speak freely; after all, Khrushchev himself had denounced Stalin's terror and the cult of his personality at the Party Congress. 'Never again,' I was told by many Russians. There were rumours that thousands of political prisoners had been set free. One could sense a general relaxation and an eagerness to get in touch with the outside, the western world, especially among the young Russians. Their favourite popular song was now 'Moscow Nights', romantic and erotic. Many people in the East and West were looking forward to a long international honeymoon, ignoring the pessimists' warning voices.

9

In fact, however, that bright picture of the world of 1960 still had a good many dark spots if one only cared to have a closer look. There were the victims of recent wars and upheavals in Europe, the Middle East, the Far East: the survivors of Hitler's holocaust, the 'displaced persons', the exiled and the dispossessed. To focus attention on these forgotten sufferers, the United Nations had declared 1960 'World Refugee Year'. But there were also millions of people displaced, dispossessed, and without civil liberties in their own countries: Czechoslovakia, once such a brave outpost of Western democracy in Eastern Europe, had reverted to harsh Stalinism, with show trials, executions, and imprisonment of dissidents. South Africa made *apartheid* its legal policy in 1948, with draconic laws to stifle disobedience and opposition. Two dictators still ruled the Iberian peninsula; Franco in Spain and Salazar in Portugal, their regimes being propped up by the military, a ubiquitous secret police, and politically corrupt judges.

One morning in November, 1960, a London lawyer was travelling by tube to his 'chambers' in the Temple. He was reading the newspaper. A short item caught his eye: a couple of Portuguese students had been arrested in a Lisbon restaurant and sentenced to seven years' imprisonment for raising their glasses in a toast to freedom.

The lawyer was thirty-nine year old Peter Benenson, of Jewish descent and mixed English-Russian parentage. He had been educated at a Church of England school and then at Eton and Oxford. After six years' service in the army he had been called to the Bar; at the age of thirty seven he had become a Catholic. He had made law reform and cases of injustice his special concern, and by the 1950s he was trying to help people persecuted for their political and religious beliefs in various countries, attending their trials as an observer or as defence counsel (usually at his own expense), writing and broadcasting about wrongs inflicted upon them by autocratic governments of every political shade. The 'treason' trials in South Africa and the prosecutions of the democratic 'rebels' in Hungary had prompted him to ask a number of his British colleagues for their active support, and they founded an all-party organization of lawyers, 'Justice', to campaign for the maintenance of the Rule of Law and the observation of Human Rights as declared by the United Nations. That had been in 1957, but little had been achieved since then — not nearly enough in the opinion of the members of 'Justice'.

Benenson's first impulse after reading the report about the two

Portuguese students was to go to the Portuguese Embassy in London and lodge a personal protest. But then he had second thoughts: What, he wondered, would be the reaction of an oppressive regime to such an individual protest, or even to that of a group of British lawyers? Salazar's underlings would drop it straight into the wastepaper basket. What was needed in such cases was a powerful barrage of world-wide protests, impressing on the dictators that international public opinion would not let them get away with acts of injustice.

Gradually, the idea of an international campaign to draw public attention to the plight of political and religious prisoners ripened in Benenson's mind. One whole year of intense pressure, he thought, could be of great benefit to the world-wide cause of justice, and save at least some of the persecuted from imprisonment, torture, or even from execution. 1961 would be a good year for such a campaign: the centenary of the liberation of slaves in America and Russia; on March 3, 1861, Tsar Alexander had signed the decree that liberated the serfs, and the next day, thousands of miles away, the new President of the United States, Abraham Lincoln, declared, 'This country belongs to the people who inhabit it.' Four years and a Civil War later, it did, at least constitutionally: slavery had ended.

The first men Benenson spoke to about his project were a fellow-lawyer, Louis Blom-Cooper Q.C., and Eric Baker, a prominent English Quaker. They agreed to cooperate. So did the members of Justice. A name for the campaign was discussed, and it was decided to call it 'Appeal for Amnesty, 1961' — perhaps a slight misnomer, for the Greek word 'amnesty' meant originally the intentional overlooking of some offence, the pardoning of the offender, while the essence of the campaign was the liberation of innocent victims. But the aims of the campaign, as formulated by Benenson and his supporters, made this clear:

1. To work impartially for the release of those imprisoned for their opinions;
2. To seek for them a fair and public trial;
3. To enlarge the Right of Asylum and help political refugees to find work;
4. To urge effective international machinery to guarantee freedom of opinion.

An office for collecting and publishing information about 'Prisoners of Conscience', as the Amnesty group termed them, was set up; in fact it was no more than a corner of Benenson's

11

own modest office in the Temple. But it had to suffice for the handful of people who formed the nucleus of the campaign — some lawyers and intellectuals, with a sprinkling of journalists and politicians — and for the voluntary secretarial helpers. A resounding opening shot for the campaign was regarded as essential. Benenson knew the editor of the British Sunday paper *The Observer*, who promised him a double-page spread of an appeal article, to be written by Benenson; a simultaneous article was to appear in the leading French paper *Le Monde*. Benenson made a further request: the article should appear on Trinity Sunday, May 28, 1961 — to give the religious day a new secular meaning. For the campaign aimed at the setting up of a 'Threes Network', whereby each group of Amnesty supporters should 'adopt' three prisoners and work for their release: one in a Communist-bloc state, one in a western country, and one in a developing country of the 'Third World'. In this way, the absolute impartiality of the campaign would be assured.

The Forgotten Prisoners

'Open your newspaper any day of the week,' began Benenson's article, 'and you will find a report from somewhere in the world of someone being imprisoned, tortured or executed because his opinions or religious beliefs are unacceptable to his government. There are several million such people in prison — by no means all of them behind the Iron and Bamboo curtains — and their numbers are growing. The newspaper reader feels a sickening sense of impotence. Yet if these feelings of disgust all over the world could be united into common action, something effective could be done.'

The article, headed 'The Forgotten Prisoners', went on to quote the U.N. Declaration of Human Rights of 1948: 'Everyone has the right to freedom of thought, conscience and religion . . . of opinion and expression. This right includes freedom to hold opinions without interference and to seek, receive and impart information and ideas through any media and regardless of frontiers.'

Noble words, signed by all the member states of the United Nations. But what mattered were not the rights that existed on paper in the countries' constitutions, but whether they were being exercised and enforced in practice. The article quoted some recent cases of blatant injustice: non-conformists were imprisoned under trumped-up charges in Franco's Spain, where students who circulated leaflets calling merely for the right to hold discussions were accused of 'military rebellion'; in Hungary, priests who tried to keep their choir schools open were charged with 'homosexuality'. But these cover-up charges showed that governments were reacting to the pressure of outside opinion. And when that pressure was concentrated on one weak spot, it could sometimes make a government relent, as in the case of the Hungarian poet Tibor Dery who had been released after the formation of 'Tibor Dery committees' in many countries; and in Spain, a professor of literature and his friends had recently been acquitted after some distinguished foreign observers had arrived to attend the trial.

'The important thing,' wrote Benenson, 'is to mobilise public opinion quickly and widely before a government is caught up in the vicious spiral caused by its own repression. . . The force of opinion, to be effective, should be broadly based, international, non-sectarian and all-party. Campaigns in favour of freedom brought by one country, or party, against another, often achieve nothing but an intensification of persecution.

'That is why we have started Appeal for Amnesty, 1961. The campaign, which opens today, is the result of an initiative by a group of lawyers, writers and publishers in London, who share the underlying conviction expressed by Voltaire: "I detest your views, but I am prepared to die for your right to express them."'

A Penguin paperback, to be published within a few weeks as part of the Amnesty campaign, was in production, wrote Benenson in his *Observer* article. He quoted some cases it would contain, such as that of Angola's leading poet, Dr. Agostino Neto, who had been treated with 'revolting brutality'. He was one of only five African doctors in that Portuguese colony, and his efforts to improve the health services for his fellow Africans were unacceptable to the colonial authorities. One day, the Political Police marched into his house, flogged him in front of his family, and then dragged him away. He was now in prison in the Cap Verde Isles without charge or trial.

Another case to be reported in the paperback was that of a Romanian philosopher, Constantin Noica, who had been sentenced to twenty-five years' imprisonment for 'conspiring against the security of the State' and 'spreading propaganda hostile to the regime'. What had he done? When 'rusticated' by his university he had allowed his friends and students to continue to visit him and listen to him reading from his own works. Then there was a Spanish lawyer, Antonio Amat, who tried to build a coalition of democratic groups and had been in prison without trial for three years. Two white men were being persecuted 'by their own race' for demanding that the coloured people should have equal rights — Ashton Jones, a sixty-five year old minister, who had been beaten up repeatedly and imprisoned three times in Louisiana and Texas, and the South African Patrick Duncan, the son of a former South African Governor-General, also thrice imprisoned because of his opposition to *apartheid.*

The American philosopher John Dewey once said, 'If you want to establish some conception of a society, go find out who is in gaol.' This, continued the *Observer* article, was hard advice to follow, because authoritarian governments do not welcome enquiries about the prisoners of conscience they are holding, and public trials before an impartial court were rare. By taking their opponents into 'preventive detention' — one of Hitler's most obnoxious practices — governments were side-stepping the needs to make and prove criminal charges.

'The most rapid way of bringing relief to prisoners of conscience,' wrote Benenson, 'is publicity, especially publicity among their fellow-citizens. With the pressure of emergent nationalism and the tensions of the Cold War, there are bound to be situations where governments are led to take emergency measures to protect their existence. It is vital that public opinion should insist that these measures should not be excessive, nor prolonged after the moment of danger. If the emergency is to last a long time, then a government should be induced to allow its opponents out of prison to seek asylum abroad . . .

'The success of the 1961 Amnesty Campaign depends on how sharply and powerfully it is possible to rally public opinion. It depends, too, upon the campaign being all-embracing in composition, international in character and politically impartial. . . . Pressure of opinion a hundred years ago brought about the emancipation of the slaves. It is now for man to insist upon the same freedom for his mind as he has won for his body.'

Half a dozen photographs of political prisoners were heading the *Observer* article, among them those of Toni Ambatielos, the Greek Communist and trade unionist, and of Cardinal Mindszenty, Primate of Hungary, who had been in gaol and was at that time a refugee trapped in the U.S. Embassy in Budapest.

Amnesty Continual
'The article evoked an unexpected number of letters, some donations, and editorial support in a large number of internationally

influential newspapers,' wrote the lawyer Peter Archer, one of the founder members of Amnesty (later he was elected Labour Member of Parliament, and eventually he became Solicitor General). Dozens of long articles appeared, apart from the coverage in *Le Monde*, in all the leading papers outside the Iron Curtain countries, from West Germany's *Die Welt* and the *New York Tribune*, from the *Journal de Genève*, Denmark's *Berlingske Tidende* and Sweden's *Politiken*, to the newspapers in Holland and Italy, South Africa and Belgium, Ireland and India, and at the risk of incurring Franco's displeasure, even a Barcelona paper published the appeal. A thousand letters arrived at the Amnesty office, many from abroad, offering help and cooperation or containing information about prisoners of conscience.

'We had underestimated the intellectual capacity and the conscience of the public,' Peter Archer continued. 'The *Observer* article also produced a harvest of offers from people in offices, schools, churches and factories. And it was here that Amnesty found its greatest source of moral strength. As the purpose was to work not for ideologies and theories, but for people, so the means was to channel the concern of people. We set up a system of local groups, consisting of neighbours, colleagues at the same workplace, or fellow worshippers at a church. They were to "adopt" individual prisoners, to write to their governments asking for their release, to send food and comforts where the authorities would permit, to raise funds to feed and educate their families and to correspond with the prisoners, assuring them that someone cared. And the impartiality which characterized the entire campaign would be safeguarded by the groups . . . The publicity on which the campaign relied might depend on the reaction to particular events and stories of many who would not extrapolate from the particular to the general. But the groups themselves must recognize the principle. A group based on, say, a Catholic church would be working for prisoners of all denominations, or of none.'

What the beginnings of the movement were like at grass-roots level has been vividly described by one of its first active supporters, Mrs. Diana Redhouse, a professional designer and housewife living in Hampstead, London's traditional quarter of artists and intellectuals. 'When I read the *Observer* appeal,' she said, 'I was horrified and upset that such terrible things were going on and one knew nothing about them. I got in touch with the address given in the article, Peter Benenson's office, asking what one could do to help.

15

I was invited to come to a meeting at Peter Archer's flat in Hampstead, with Mrs. Archer acting as the secretary. The outcome was that we formed Amnesty's very first adoption group, just two other women and myself, all of us living in that area. We decided to hold a "mass" meeting in aid of those Forgotten Prisoners. Twenty people came, and we collected three pounds and ten shillings. A little later we arranged a "Bring-and-Buy" sale at my house. We raised five pounds.'

It was a characteristically English, almost parochial beginning, made by people who felt that something ought to be done, and who were prepared to devote their time, energy and money to it.

Benenson spoke to Diana Redhouse about his idea to design an emblem for Amnesty, epitomizing the spirit of the movement: a candle flame burning amidst barbed wire. He was thinking of an old Chinese proverb, 'Better light a candle than curse the darkness' — in other words: better do something than nothing. Mrs. Redhouse designed that Amnesty candle as a simple yet effective and powerful symbol. It has remained the movement's emblem to this day (although there have been a few objections that the candle might be seen as a religious symbol).

A real, outsize Anmesty candle was lit for the first time on Human Rights Day in December, 1961, on the steps of the church St. Martin's-in-the-Fields, in London's Trafalgar Square, by Odette Churchill-Hallowes, the World War II heroine. She had been a British agent in German-occupied France, was captured by the *Gestapo*, tortured and sent to a concentration camp, but escaped. In her hands the flame in barbed wire was the symbol not only for all prisoners of conscience, but also of their hope of survival and freedom.

One of the first Amnesty branches to be founded outside England was the West German one — no doubt the country's recent history of dictatorship and oppression had made its younger generation particularly concerned about human rights. Carola Stern, editor of a large publishing house (later with the West German Radio), and the journalist Gerd Ruge (later China correspondent of *Die Welt*) started organizing Amnesty in the Federal Republic, with Cologne as the centre. They got their first three prisoners for adoption, selected according to the basic Amnesty principle of impartiality: a poet in Soviet Russia, a Jehovah's Witness in Spain, a Communist writer in South Africa. Local adoption groups were soon formed in Hamburg and Munich.

The world-wide response to the *Observer* article, the many

enquiries from sympathizers asking how they could help the campaign best in their own countries made it an urgent necessity to call an international meeting. The first assembly of delegates took place at a café in Luxembourg in July, 1961, a mere eight weeks after Trinity Sunday, with delegates from Britain, France, Belgium, Ireland, Switzerland, and the USA. It was at this meeting that the suggestion was made, almost as a matter of course, to turn the one-year appeal campaign into 'a permanent international movement in defence of freedom of opinion and religion'. As Benenson put it: the response to the appeal had shown that even in a cynical age there was a great, latent well of idealism, waiting to be tapped, but a single short trumpet blast would not make the prison walls come tumbling down. The new name of the movement, officially adopted in the following year, was to be 'Amnesty International', AI for short; and its basis in all countries should, of course, be the adoption groups of active supporters. Despite its semantic blemish, 'Amnesty' *was* the best name for the movement: it is identical, or nearly so, in most languages.

One important point had already begun to emerge: that there need be no fear about writing openly to prisoners of conscience regarding the activities to get them released, or at least tried in open court. Even if a letter is confiscated and never reaches the prisoner, it will be read by government officials or prison authorities. The realization that these prisoners are not forgotten, that there are in other countries people who care for them may already result in an improvement in their treatment. Another point, which was laid down as a necessary restriction at that early stage of the movement, was that the groups should never adopt prisoners held in their own countries. Nor could Amnesty ever take up cases of prisoners who had used or advocated violence.

Collecting money was recognized as an essential task for the groups. Apart from helping to maintain the whole organization, funds were needed for sending defence lawyers or observers to trials, and investigators to the countries where prisoners were held; and the groups' main tasks, of course, were to write, and mail gift parcels, to the men and women they had adopted, and send money to their families who were often living in poverty after losing their bread-winners.

Among the national groups and sections founded already in the second half of 1961 were, apart from that in the German Federal Republic, those in Belgium, Switzerland (groups in Zurich and Geneva), Greece, Australia (after Benenson had been

17

interviewed for five minutes in a BBC World Service broadcast from London), the United States (he allayed the State Department's suspicion that Amnesty was a 'red plot' during a visit in September), New Zealand, South Africa, Canada, Nigeria, Sudan, Ghana, Iraq, Burma, India, Yugoslavia, South Korea, and even in rigidly authoritarian countries like Czechoslovakia, Spain and Portugal. One of the earliest national sections was that in the Irish Republic.

Ireland's greatest contribution to Amnesty was one man — Sean MacBride. He was the son of Major John MacBride, a passionate resistance fighter who had been executed by the British after the 1916 Easter Rising; his mother was the almost legendary Maud Gonne, the 'patron-saint' of Ireland's oppressed. As a teenager, Sean MacBride was also imprisoned, and so was his mother. He became a lawyer, founded the Irish Republican Party, and entered the Dublin Parliament; in 1948 he was Foreign Minister. His deep concern for human rights and justice — he was a leading member of the International Commission of Jurists — brought him into contact with Benenson, and together they planned the first 'missions' to help individual prisoners, thrashing out tactics which Amnesty was to use in subsequent years.*

The Case of Archbishop Beran

In his *Observer* appeal, Benenson had recalled the case of the Archbishop of Prague, Josef Beran. As a middle-aged priest he had spoken up against the Nazis, then the occupants of Czechoslovakia, and was taken to the concentration camps of Dachau and Theresienstadt. But after the Communist coup of 1948, he fell out with the new rulers of his country. In 1949, the police raided his house; and after a last, defiant sermon he was arrested as he was leaving Prague's St. Vitus cathedral. The next news about the Archbishop came in 1951; he had been 'deposed' at a large-scale treason trial, evicted from his diocese, and a fine had been imposed on him. From then on, nothing more was heard about him; rumours said he was under house arrest at a disused monastery, that he was seriously ill or even dead.

His case was one of the first taken up by Amnesty. Benenson wrote an open letter to the Czechoslovak Ambassador in London, Amnesty groups in other countries also wrote to the Czech ambassadors. There was practically no response. Amnesty sent a repre-

*Sean MacBride was awarded the Nobel Prize for Peace in 1974.

18

sentative to the London embassy; he was told that Beran was not in prison, that he was being cared for by nuns and in good health. His whereabouts were not disclosed — 'He doesn't want to be disturbed by foreign reporters,' was the threadbare explanation.

Now MacBride went into action. Benenson got the Catholic family newspaper, *Universe*, to pay for MacBride to go to Prague in February, 1962. The former Irish Foreign Minister was received by his colleague Jiri Hajek, of the Czechoslovak Foreign Ministry, who was polite but evasive. MacBride's request to see the Archbishop was refused. He insisted: would the Czech authorities permit a visit by some independent observer? At last he got the promise that the authorities would think this over. 'I pointed out,' wrote MacBride in his report to Amnesty, 'that it was in the interest of Czechoslovakia to reassure the world that its new constitution of 1960 heralded a new era of freedom. I found that this direct argument had some influence, and I left feeling more hopeful about the future.'

However, more than a year and a half passed without any results. So Amnesty stepped up its campaign. Beran was put at the head of its list of 'forgotten prisoners'. Meetings demanding his release were held in many western countries. The media cooperated; short-wave broadcasts beamed at Eastern Europe told the story of the Archbishop. It is, of course, difficult to gauge the effect of that campaign on the minds of the Prague rulers. At any rate, in October, 1963, the Archbishop and four other bishops who had also been imprisoned were set free, at least to some extent: Beran was still kept under house arrest at a Catholic hostel near Prague and banned from carrying out his religious duties, and his request that he should be allowed to visit Rome was not granted. However, a letter of thanks for Amnesty's help in 'having me freed' reached London in November, 1963. 'I pray for Amnesty International,' he wrote. 'I pray for all who support Amnesty.'

In the summer of 1964, a Danish Amnesty representative went to Czechoslovakia to find out what had happened to a number of prisoners of conscience, and he was permitted to see Beran, who told him that he was now free to move about — so long as he did not go to Prague, or get in touch with any Church institutions. He sent Amnesty his renewed blessing. Early in 1965, Pope Paul VI made him a Cardinal; a few weeks later, he was at last permitted to leave for Rome (where he stayed until his death in 1969, at the age of eighty-one). In 1966 he came to London to express personally his gratitude to AI, taking part in a ceremony at which he lit the 'Amnesty Candle' as the symbol of remembrance of prisoners of conscience all over the world.

Beran's case was important for the movement also because it underlined a basic lesson: Amnesty must never boast of some particular success in helping to free prisoners, especially in totalitarian countries. Apart from the difficulty of producing evidence that the movement had been directly responsible for their liberation, any such boast would annoy or embarrass the government concerned and antagonise it against future intervention by Amnesty. This does not mean, of course, that AI should refrain from publicizing evidence about the state of prisoners in such countries, and from demanding their release with the help of the media. But for similar reasons, even the individual, often private ways in which AI representatives − called 'investigators' − had to approach their tasks could not always be disclosed. One principle, however, was to be rigidly upheld: there must be no secret deals with foreign authorities concerning prisoners, and no exchanges of prisoners as governments in the East and West sometimes arrange them − less for humane considerations than for reasons of political expediency.

The last month of 1961 brought a formidable and imaginative action in which supporters and sympathizers of Amnesty everywhere could take part. Five thousand Amnesty Christmas cards, with quotations on freedom in six languages, were printed and sold; with each batch of twenty cards, supporters received a list of twelve prisoners in gaols all over the world to whom they could be sent. Senders and AI head office received quite a number of letters of thanks from prisoners, who said that the cards had brought them much hope and comfort.

Amnesty's accountants published the balance sheet of the movement for the first twelve months of its existence. The sum total of its turnover was ridiculously small, compared to the importance and influence it had already achieved − £7,859, with over £1,000 to hand in cash and in the bank. Nearly all the income had been from subscriptions and donations.

Four Amnesty investigators took up their work early in 1962, travelling with financial assistance from newspapers. Sean MacBride was one of them; another was the British lawyer Louis Blom-Cooper, who went to Ghana to obtain information about opponents of the increasingly despotic Nkrumah regime, imprisoned under the Preventive Detention Act of 1958. (Without claiming this as a success, Amnesty reported five months later that one hundred and fifty-two detainees had been released in that country).

Neville Vincent, a London barrister who had also been associated with Amnesty right from the start and was now Joint Honorary Secretary, travelled to Portugal to intercede with the Salazar government on behalf of some doctors imprisoned for their political beliefs. Vincent was refused entry, but six months later Archbishop Roberts was received by Cardinal Cerejeira, head of Portugal's Catholic hierarchy, and a close friend of Salazar. The Cardinal promised to pass on Roberts' representations to the Prime Minister.

A few weeks later, three of the doctors were released.

The Case of Heinz Brandt

Investigator Prem Khera, an Indian lawyer and trade-unionist, visited East Germany — the 'German Democratic Republic' (GDR), as it calls itself — in March, 1962, to investigate three cases. Heinz Brandt, a fellow trade-unionist, had disappeared from West Germany — he was now in gaol in the GDR, awaiting trial. A forestry expert, Dr. Rohrig, had been imprisoned for unknown reasons; and an eighteen-year-old student, Jürgen Wiechert, had been given a gaol sentence of eight years merely for protesting to the captain of a holiday cruise ship about an unexplained change of route.

Khera had a long talk with the East German Attorney General, who assured him that should Amnesty want to send an observer to Heinz Brandt's trial, every facility would be offered. This turned out to be an empty promise; the trial was held in secret, and all that was reported about it was that Brandt had been sentenced to thirteen and a half years of hard labour as an enemy of the state.

Wiechert was cared for by an adoption group in Harrow, near London, who bombarded the GDR authorities with letters of protest. After serving two years in gaol, he was released. In Heinz Brandt's case, obviously a highly political one, stronger action seemed necessary. He was made Amnesty's Prisoner of the Year for 1963.

Brandt was the third prisoner to be 'honoured' with this unenviable title. The first, in 1961, had been a stateless South African, Christopher Payi, who had been arrested for some unknown reason when travelling through Portuguese Guinea. The Prisoner of the Year scheme was not supposed to draw attention to any particular case as most deserving of help, but as a symbol for the cases of hundreds of thousands of other prisoners. The publicity Payi got in this way seemed to have helped; he was set free after a few months in gaol — one of one hundred and forty prisoners released out of seven hundred and seventy adopted by Amnesty in 1962-63. His successor as Prisoner of the Year for 1962 was Abdul Ghaffar Khan, the seventy-two year old leader of a religious/ nationalist movement in the north-west of Pakistan, imprisoned since 1947, the year of Pakistan's independence. His 'crime' was that he had demanded autonomy for the four million Pathans, a group of warlike and freedom-loving tribes living in that area. Amnesty launched an intensive campaign on his behalf, and he was freed in 1964.

Heinz Brandt's case made him particularly 'eligible' as Prisoner of the Year, not only because the GDR authorities had blatantly flouted the promises given to Khera by the Attorney General but because of the severity of his sentence. This trade-unionist had been in concentration camps under Hitler throughout the whole twelve years of Nazi rule. There was no doubt that he had been abducted; he had been drinking a glass of whisky with friends in West Berlin — and woke up in an East Berlin prison cell.

An independent 'mission' to try and get him released was undertaken by a churchman who could speak German, the Rev. Paul Oestreicher. Born in Germany, he had been an eight year old refugee when his parents emigrated with him to New Zealand in 1939. Twenty years later, he moved to England; he had graduated in political science, published books on Christianity and Marxism, and eventually turned to the study of theology. He was ordained to Anglican priesthood in 1959, but continued to work as a writer and journalist; in 1961 he became a producer of religious programmes on BBC Radio, and made the first major feature on Amnesty. (In 1974, Oestreicher was elected Chairman of the British Section of Amnesty International.)

His mission to East Germany in 1963 — when he was active for the British Council of Churches — had been preceded by a vigorous campaign for Brandt's release in which Bertrand Russell took a major part — the great philosopher warned the East Germans that he would return the 'Ossietzky Medal' they had awarded to him for his services to world peace if they kept the trade union leader much longer in prison. They did not react, and Oestreicher went to East Berlin together with John Collins, the Canon of St. Paul's and co-founder of the Campaign for Nuclear

Disarmament. They spoke to Walter Ulbricht, top man of the GDR establishment, who merely said that Brandt was 'justly imprisoned', but he would 'look into the case'.

On Human Rights Day in December 1963, Brandt's wife was invited to light the Amnesty Candle at a solemn ceremony in St. Bride's, the church of Fleet Street. Heinz Brandt was at last released in May, 1964, and returned to West Germany. On Human Rights Day of that year, it was he who lit the Amnesty Candle in London.

Amnesty's first Crisis

Another East German prisoner adopted by an Irish group was Peter Hermann, who had been sentenced to 14 years' penal servitude as a student of twenty-three in 1958 for 'activities against the state'. The group wrote constantly to members of the GDR government about him, and also to the governor of the Brandenburg prison where he was kept. 'I did not know anything about your letters,' he told 'his' group in Ireland after his release in 1964. 'But I was surprised that suddenly some of the requests I had made were granted: I got permission to write in my cell, I got my own books for studying; and I was driven to Jena, where my mother was on her deathbed — a thing that had never before happened to a political prisoner. I did not know why I was singled out for these privileges, but I think it is possible that this was due to your efforts.' He thought that there were still ten thousand prisoners of conscience in East Germany.

A seventeen-year-old Basque mechanic, Fermin Elola, was also adopted by an Irish group after he had been arrested and imprisoned in April, 1964 in Madrid as a member of the Basque resistance movement. A big flag of the movement had been hoisted in Zarauz, Elola's home town. The adoption group spent months trying to find out whether he had had any kind of trial. Some letters were sent to the Spanish Ambassador in Dublin and to the prison governor, asking to have Elola included in a partial amnesty by Franco to mark the 25th anniversary of the end of the Civil War. Early in December, the group was informed that Elola had been set free.

Perhaps it was the general atmosphere of compassion fostered by Amnesty which moved some governments to decide on large-scale releases. On Human Rights Day, 1963, Eire freed thirty-seven prisoners; in the summer of 1964, Romania was reported to have set several thousand political prisoners free, and Greece,

Egypt, and Burma acted on similar lines. Salazar's Portugal, however, seemed unaffected by what Amnesty had hoped was a world-wide humanitarian trend. In July, 1964, a monster trial was staged in Lisbon against eighty-six people charged with having been connected with an abortive rebellion two years before. Sixty-five of them were sent to prison for up to ten years.

The same year brought Amnesty's first internal crisis, centred on one prisoner — Nelson Mandela, the black South African lawyer and politician. Born in 1918, the son of a tribal chief in the Transkei, he joined the African National Congress in 1944 and headed a non-violent campaign against the *apartheid* laws in 1952. The Pretoria government imposed restriction of movement on him and banned him from attending any meetings. He was charged with high treason in 1956, but acquitted. These experiences turned Mandela from a convinced pacifist into an activist who founded, in 1961, a militant movement which was to prepare for an armed rebellion. In 1962, he was arrested again, and sentenced to five years in prison. But in 1964 he was imprisoned for life. The charge was sabotage.

Mandela had been adopted as a prisoner of conscience so long as the charges against him were merely that he had tried to organize a strike and to leave the country without a passport. Early in 1963, Amnesty sent him books to help him study in prison for a degree. Ten months later, he passed his LL.B as an external student in the intermediary section of London University. By that time, however, he was branded as a militant activist, and his British adoption group ceased to work for his release.

This was a major question of fundamental principles for the Amnesty members. A poll among them was arranged; the main question put to them was whether AI should in future work for the release of prisoners who had used or advocated violent means in pursuance of the aims of their racial groups. The result was announced and discussed at an AI meeting in Canterbury in September, 1964. The overwhelming majority of members' replies, endorsed by one hundred delegates from all over the world, reaffirmed the basic Amnesty rule that prisoners who had used or advocated violence should not be adopted. The exception were cases of self-defence, or symbolic acts like tearing down flags or defacing posters. But the meeting felt that to abandon Mandela now that he was a prisoner on the notorious Robben Island would be inhuman, and to fail a victim of repression when he most needed support would be to go against the spirit of

Amnesty. So a compromise was reached in the form of a resolution declaring that, although Mandela would no longer remain a prisoner of conscience, the movement might, on humanitarian grounds, make representations relating to the sentence or conditions of detention of *any* prisoner.

The Canterbury meeting was memorable also for various other items on its agenda. It was decided to appeal to all governments 'not to carry out death sentences for political offences until six months after sentence, or until an appeal to a higher court has been heard'. The Annual Report for 1963/4, which had been published with an introduction by a great supporter of Amnesty, Dr. Albert Schweitzer, disclosed that out of one thousand three hundred and sixty-seven prisoners adopted during the first three years, three hundred and twenty-nine had been released; there were now three hundred and sixty groups in fourteen countries — and the AI budget had risen to £10,000.

The first Canadian AI group was now in operation. A branch was also founded in Israel; the 'grand old man' of Zionism, Professor Martin Buber, was an enthusiastic Amnesty supporter. So was Bishop Martin Niemöller in Germany, the man who had been one of the Kaiser's Uboat captains in World War I, then turned pacifist and became a hero of the anti-Nazi resistance. He had spent eight years in Hitler's concentration camps. Now, as President of the World Council of Churches, he called Amnesty 'a light shining in a world of darkness and inhumanity'.

The most important personnel change was that Peter Benenson, until then Secretary-General to the International Executive Committee, was elected President of AI; this was done to relieve him of the most time-consuming administrative jobs. Jack Halpern, a former South African journalist, was appointed Secretary-General.

A Painter's Trip to Haiti

Benenson had perhaps overtaxed his strength; he was now in his mid-forties and not a very healthy man. At any rate, when he addressed the Canterbury meeting, he did so in a pessimistic mood which seemed out of character with the man who had started a highly successful movement. But he did not feel that it had come up to expectations: 'Torture and intimidation are growing in the world,' he said. 'A thousand people have possibly been executed in Baghdad from motives of revenge after the last change of government there — and we can't do anything about it. We have

25

made no impact at all! The prisoners adopted by Amnesty International are only a small proportion of the prisoners of conscience throughout the world; there are great numbers we will never be able to know about.'

Had the delegates come from far and wide to be depressed by such words? Sean MacBride obviously felt that they could now do with a spell of uplift. He spoke about the large-scale release of prisoners of conscience in Eastern Europe and in Spain, and then he added, 'Although it cannot be said that the release of two or three thousand people was the actual work of Amnesty International, its influence is obvious.'

The listeners may have sensed that the two men were no longer seeing eye to eye about the movement. These differences of opinion were to become even more marked within a year or two.

Benenson — who had retired from the Bar altogether — had been incredibly active for the movement. He had visited most of the universities, which were a particularly fertile ground for Amnesty; there was special enthusiasm for the movement at Oxford, where a dozen active groups had been established already by 1962. He kept in constant touch with the groups and sections in Scandinavia, as a 'follow-up' to the great interest AI had found there. Sweden had been the first country to publish Benenson's *Persecution 1961* in its own language, and its national section had grown into the relatively strongest of all sections outside Britain.

Benenson's most memorable journey was that to Haiti in 1964; it was also a dangerous one because he wanted to obtain information about 'Papa Doc's' political prisoners, to be published in an Amnesty report. The dicator François Duvalier's nickname stemmed from the time when he was still a country doctor, trying to raise the dreadful living conditions of the Haitian poor. This was his original reason for entering politics, but his character seemed to have changed completely when he became a member of the military junta which took over the government after the previous dictator had been deposed in 1956. A year later, Duvalier was elected President, and within a short period his regime became much more corrupt, oppressive, and murderous than that of his predecessor; he resorted to mass arrests, torture, and even to voodoo to stifle opposition and stay in power. In 1961, Britain and the U.S. protested against his attempts to extort money from their nationals living in Haiti; two years later came a crisis in the form of a confrontation with the Dominican Republic — it occupies the eastern two-thirds of the island — but Duvalier survived it and declared himself President for Life in 1962.

A new crisis (which was to lead to a much criticised American armed intervention in the Dominican Republic) was still in its early stages when Benenson arrived in Haiti. He had been travelling as a tourist; to be precise: as an artist intending to paint the natural beauty of the island, and under that camouflage he was allowed to enter. In fact, painting had always been Benenson's great hobby. Duvalier's secret police kept an eye on him, and in order to avoid their suspicion he had to be rather busy with his brushes, especially in the early hours of the morning and at dusk — he needed the rest of the day for clandestine interviews with Duvalier's victims and their families. The police, who visited him from time to time, were shown masses of pictures he had painted.

He got the material he needed for his report, and departed without hindrance. But when the report was published, the story of his disguise came out, Duvalier made a furious protest to the British ambassador in Haiti, and Benenson was asked to account for his action. He retorted, 'It's no use trying to placate dictators.' In fact, the British Ambassador was sent packing by Duvalier a few months later, and the embassy closed down.

The Benenson report on Haiti was one of the major documents deposited with Amnesty's new Research Department, which had been established at the end of 1963. Its Prisoner of Conscience Library had already files on two thousand eight hundred cases from eighty-three countries, which were constantly being brought up to date and filled up with background information by a wide international network of voluntary researchers.

The Research Department and other new features of the movement had been introduced as a result of the discussions at Königswinter, the idyllic German tourist centre on the Rhine, where Amnesty delegates from many countries met in the autumn of 1963. Here, it was decided to set up a separate International Secretariat, supervised by a five-man International Executive; the Five were elected on a linguistic basis: from English-, French-, German-, Dutch-, and Scandinavian-speaking areas. Sean MacBride was elected Chairman, Benenson Honorary International Secretary. It was also decided to establish an Investigation Department 'to find out more about those cases of imprisonment which appear to fall within the prisoner of conscience definition', all information to be collected on case sheets. If details were lacking, volunteers should be asked to try and discover the circumstances of arrest, the charge (if any), the address of the prison and of the prisoner's next-of-kin.

The Research Department was set up to centralize the earlier, somewhat uncoordinated efforts of helping prisoners. This department was now to receive and check the cases of prisoners of conscience, reported to Amnesty by supporters, relatives, friends, or by the media, before passing them on to the adoption groups Previously, the groups had been given the name of a 'contact' for each prisoner, to whom they could write for further information and advice, but with the increase of the number of groups – from seventy in 1962 to three hundred and sixty in 1964 – the time and resources of many contacts were in danger of exhaustion. So it was decided that the Research Department should prepare a 'background paper' on each country where prisoners were being held, to be sent to the groups, together with the case sheets prepared by the International Secretariat. The background papers should contain information about the political and religious situation, the types of prisoners, the prison conditions, the best means of making contact with the prisoners and their families, and there should also be a list of names of influential people in the country concerned, who might be approached with requests to support pleas for clemency.

The 'Kit Scheme'

The whole atmosphere among the supporters of the movement was changing; it was growing up, and its youthful *élan* was giving way to a readiness for steady practical work, conscientious and reliable. The Honorary International Secretary, writing in the Annual Report for 1964-65, described the change in these words: 'During the first three years the movement was carried forward by a surge of initial enthusiasm. Numbers of people all over the world, infected with this enthusiasm, offered their help. It has taken the twin tests of time and hard work to show which offers can be permanently relied upon. During this fourth year a cadre of devoted Amnesty workers has begun to develop. These are the men and women of greatly differing ages and conditions of life who have come to understand the underlying philosophy and the techniques of the movement. Those who thought that they were joining a mass demonstration in favour of freedom in its widest anarchical sense have dropped away. So have those who saw this movement as a weapon to be added to the armoury of their own political cause.'

Somehow, the Prisoner of the Year scheme seemed at odds with this new spirit. To be sure, it had proved useful in highlighting the fate of all the men and women deprived of their freedom because of their convictions, and it also served as a means of making the media write and talk about AI by giving them a 'news' story. But, as one critic put it, the scheme was 'too much like a beauty contest'.

The Prisoner of the Year selected in December, 1964, was Julieta Gandra in Portugal, imprisoned since 1959 for 'plotting against the internal security of the State'. Soon after the usual London church ceremony publicising her case she was released. The next Prisoner of the Year was a teacher in Guinea, Madou Ray-Autra Traore, sentenced to five years in prison for merely opposing the nationalisation of the education system in his country. The conditions in his prison were reported to be 'very bad'. However, his selection as Prisoner of the Year had hardly been publicised when the news came that Traore had already been freed before the church ceremony. AI had to apologize for its activity on his behalf. It was a most embarrassing incident, which may have contributed to the decision to abandon the Prisoner of the Year scheme.

In a way, the 'Kit Scheme', as it was called at first, was its successor. This new feature of Amnesty's activities, which started in May, 1965, was initially designed to meet the growing interest in the United States, where many supporters encountered difficulties in forming adoption groups and, therefore, wanted to play active roles as individuals. Soon, however, the scheme proved to be successful also in other countries − not only in those where national sections existed already but, even more encouragingly, in countries where AI had previously made little headway.

It got its name from the 'kit' which was sent to supporters at their request. This consisted of a cardboard container with a handbook on AI, stating its aims and the techniques which should be used. There were also thirty-six cards − thirty-three Amnesty greeting cards and three Christmas cards. The handbook gave advice on the type of messages that should be written on them, varying according to the country and kind of addressee to whom they were to be sent − to the Head of State, to ministers, prison governors, the prisoner's family, the prisoner himself. The handbook also informed the supporter on the political histories of the countries concerned. Each month the kit-holder received a Newsletter, naming three topical cases for immediate card-writing. These prisoners' circumstances, and the reasons for the urgent appeals, were set out in detail. 'The idea of the scheme,' said AI, 'is to build up numbers and distribution of kit-holders in such a way that governments are eventually deluged by cards from everywhere.'

Today the scheme is still fully active, but it is now called the 'Prisoners of the Month Campaign'. It has also changed its character in so far as appeals should be sent only to the 'officials named at the end of each case story — in no circumstances should communications be sent to the prisoner himself (this remains the job of the adoption groups). The messages to the authorities must be worded 'carefully and courteously', and they must never be sectarian.

Altogether, 1965 was a year of intense activity. The number of prisoners under adoption had risen to one thousand two hundred (and the total of prisoners released since 1961 to eight hundred). AI appeared at the August forum of the United Nations to sponsor a resolution for the suspension and eventual abolition of capital punishment for peacetime political offences. AI was also represented at the *Palais des Nations* in Geneva and at the European Court in Strasbourg. Good relations had been established with the International Red Cross and the International Commission of Jurists as well as with organizations representing the trade unions, the students, the churches, the war veterans of many countries, and the various Human Rights associations in America; there were even promising contacts with lawyers' organizations in Eastern Europe. Also 1965 brought what Peter Archer called the 'ultimate accolade' — AI was granted consultative status with the Council of Europe (also in Strasbourg). Thus Amnesty's representatives were now occupying 'seats at the world's top tables'.

An Emergency Fund was set up for financing lawyers' journeys to attend trials at which death sentences were likely to be passed. If possible, these lawyers should know the language of the countries concerned. The aim was to get them officially admitted as observers; experience showed that the authorities in many countries would stall, but they hardly ever refused outright. As observers they had to try and speak to the lawyers involved in the trials, to the authorities, and if possible to the prisoners. The information they brought back was published as AI reports and immediately passed on to the adoption groups who cared for the prisoners on trial. The presence of AI observers may have restrained courts from passing death sentences.

In Nigeria, the trial against people supposed to have been involved in a recent army coup was imminent; Sir Learie Constantine, the former test cricketer and West Indian diplomat, undertook the journey to Lagos for Amnesty. After Rhodesia had announced UDI ('Unilateral Declaration of Independence') in November, 1965, there were reports of widespread arrests. Amnesty worker Polly Toynbee, the nineteen-year-old daughter of the writer Phillip Toynbee and grand-daughter of the historian Sir Arnold, flew to Salisbury to help the families of black supporters of Britain. Though she got a two-months visa, she was expelled after five weeks and flew to South Africa. She was not allowed to leave Jan Smuts airport, but an officer of the political police told her she could enter the country 'if I became a police informer', reporting on members of the African National Council. She refused, of course, and was sent back to London.

Amnesty was in the South Africans' bad books because it had just (in September, 1965) published a report on their prisons. 'Would that such a report had been published about Germany after the Nazis took power in 1933,' said the foreword. 'To those who may object that most of the evidence comes from former prisoners and therefore cannot be trusted, one answer is that conditions in Hitler's Auschwitz and Stalin's Vorkuta were found to be worse than any description previously given by those who had escaped.' The South African Embassy in London reacted by declaring that it 'would not entertain any future communications with Amnesty International'. The report was banned from publication in South Africa, but it did of course reach the government and the prison authorities.

Exit the 'Godfather'
Since its beginnings Amnesty's files on prisoners, later called the Prisoner of Conscience Library, had been crammed, with the staff working on it, into the basement of Benenson's London chambers at Mitre Court. But now the pioneer days had ended, and it urgently needed more space. It was moved to larger premises, together with the International Secretariat, in 1965. This cost more money, of course, and AI's financial situation was not yet a very healthy one; the 1965-66 budget was a mere £7,000. The International Secretariat needed larger means for its world-wide activities and kept turning to the national sections for help. In turn the sections asked their groups to collect money for the central fund, but the group members often replied that they needed every penny they could collect for their adopted prisoners. Financial disaster loomed large. But worse was still to come.

The latter part of 1966 brought a critical situation which was all the more shattering as it was unexpected in an organization that was now commanding attention and respect in all continents and at the highest international level. Heads of State seemed concerned not to fall out with AI, as an incident of the summer of 1966 showed. Nils Groth, a Danish lawyer and Amnesty's representative with the United Nations, went to Guinea to inquire about prisoners of conscience. He was arrested shortly after his arrival by over-zealous police officials, and kept in prison for three months without being charged. When the trial took place at last, he was sentenced to ten years' hard labour for alleged espionage — but within twenty-four hours, President Sekou Touré declared a special amnesty for him, and he was released.

It was another Scandinavian Amnesty worker who, innocently enough, triggered off a serious Amnesty crisis. He was Dr. Selahaddin Rastgeldi from Sweden, but not a native of that country. Born in Turkey of Kurdish parents, he had come to Scandinavia as a refugee from a persecuted minority and was, therefore, much concerned about prisoners of conscience, particularly in the Middle East. In 1966, the Swedish Amnesty section sent him to Aden, the former British Crown Colony which had joined the Federation of South Arabia three years earlier.

There was much trouble in Aden at the time. A hand-grenade had been thrown at the British High Commissioner, missing him but killing two people and injuring fifty; bombs and bullets had caused many casualties among the British troops. A state of emergency was declared, mass arrests were made, and many political prisoners and suspected terrorists were kept in camps indefinitely without charge. To send a British Amnesty investigator would have been wrong and might have prejudiced his credibility, so Rastgeldi was entrusted with the mission. His report, alleging maltreatment and violence used by British soldiers and British-employed Adenis, was most incriminating.

At once, British public opinion was roused against him by the press. His ethnic origins, it was said, made him unreliable. He was pro-Arab and, it was hinted, in the Egyptian President Nasser's pay. The media would not believe what he wrote in his report about having been prevented from visiting the British-run internment camps to verify reports of ill-treatment of suspects by British interrogators. Amnesty in London had tried in vain to get these facilities from the Foreign Office, and the High Commissioner in Aden told Rastgeldi he was not interested in co-

1. Peter Benenson

THE OBSERVER WEEKEND REVIEW

London, Sunday, May 28, 1961 21

SIX POLITICAL PRISONERS: left, Constantin Noica, the philosopher, now in a Rumanian gaol; centre, the Rev. Ashton Jones, friend of the Negroes, recently in gaol in the United States; right, Agostino Neto, Angolan poet and doctor, held without trial by the Portuguese. Their cases are described in the article below.

Left, Archbishop Beran of Prague, held in custody by the Czechs; centre, Tony Ambatielos, the Greek Communist and trade unionist prisoner, whose wife is English; right Cardinal Mindszenty, Primate of Hungary, formerly a prisoner and now a political refugee trapped in the United States Embassy, Budapest.

ON BOTH SIDES of the Iron Curtain, thousands of men and women are being held in gaol without trial because their political or religious views differ from those of their Governments. Peter Benenson, a London lawyer, conceived the idea of a world campaign, APPEAL FOR AMNESTY, 1961, to urge Governments to release these people or at least give them a fair trial. The campaign opens to-day, and "The Observer" is glad to offer it a platform.

The Forgotten Prisoners

OPEN your newspaper any day of the week and you will find a report from somewhere in the world of someone being imprisoned, tortured or executed because his opinions or religion are unacceptable to his government. There are several million such people in prison—by no means all of them behind the Iron and Bamboo Curtains—and their numbers are growing. The newspaper reader feels a sickening sense of impotence. Yet if these feelings of disgust all over the world could be united into common action, something effective could be done.

In 1945 the founder members of the United Nations approved the Universal Declaration of Human Rights:—

Article 18.—Everyone has the right to freedom of thought, conscience and religion; this right includes freedom to change his religion or belief, and freedom either alone or in community with others in public or private, to manifest his religion or belief in teaching, practice, worship and observance.

Article 19.—Everyone has the right to freedom of opinion and expression; this right includes freedom to hold opinions without interference and to seek, receive and impart information and ideas through any media and regardless of frontiers.

There is at present no sure way of finding out how many countries permit their citizens to enjoy these two fundamental freedoms. What matters is not the rights that exist on paper in the Constitution, but whether they can be exercised and enforced in practice. No government, for instance, is at greater pains to emphasise its constitutional guarantees than the Spanish, but it fails to apply them.

There is a growing tendency all over the world to disguise the real grounds upon which "non-conformists" are imprisoned. In Spain, students who circulate leaflets calling for the right to hold discussions on current affairs are charged with "military rebellion." In Hungary, Catholic priests who have tried to keep their choir schools open have been charged with "homosexuality." These cover-up charges indicate that governments are by no means insensitive to the pressure of outside opinion. And when world opinion is concentrated on one weak spot, it can sometimes succeed in making a government relent. For instance, the Hungarian poet Tibor Dery was recently released after the formation of "Tibor Dery committees" in many countries, and Professor Tierno Galvan and his literary friends were acquitted in Spain this March, after the arrival of some distinguished foreign observers.

London office to gather facts

The important thing is to mobilise public opinion quickly, and widely, before a government is caught up in the vicious spiral caused by its own repression, and is faced with impending civil war. By then the situation will have become too desperate for the government to make concessions. The force of opinion, to be effective, should be broadly based, international, non-sectarian and all-party. Campaigns in favour of freedom brought by one country, or party, against another, often achieve nothing but an intensification of persecution.

That is why we have started Appeal for Amnesty, 1961. The campaign, which opens to-day, is the result of an initiative by a group of lawyers, writers and publishers in London, who share the underlying conviction expressed by Voltaire: "I detest your views, but am prepared to die for your right to express them." We have set up an office in London to collect information about the names, numbers and conditions of what we have decided to call "Prisoners of Conscience," and we define them thus: "Any person who is physically restrained (by imprisonment or otherwise) from expressing (in any form of words or symbols) any opinion which he honestly holds and which does not advocate or condone personal violence." We also exclude those who have conspired with a foreign government to overthrow their own. Our office will from time to time hold Press conferences to focus attention on Prisoners of Conscience selected impartially from different parts of the world. And it will provide factual information to any group, existing or new, in any part of the world, which decides to join in a special effort in favour of freedom of opinion or religion.

In October a Penguin Special called "Persecution 1961" will be published as part of our Amnesty campaign. In it are stories of nine men and women from different parts of the world, of varying political and religious outlook, who have been suffering imprisonment for expressing their opinions. None of them is a professional politician; all of them are professional people. The opinions which have brought them to prison are the common coinage of argument in free society.

Poet flogged in front of family

One story is of the revolting brutality with which Angola's leading poet, Agostino Neto, was treated before the present disturbances there broke out. Dr. Neto was one of the few African doctors in Angola. His efforts to improve the health services for his fellow Africans were unacceptable to the Portuguese. In June last year the Political Police marched into his house, had him flogged in front of his family and then dragged away. He has since been in prison in the Cape Verde Isles without charge or trial.

From Rumania, we shall print the story of Constantin Noica, the philosopher, who was sentenced to twenty-five years' imprisonment because, while "rusticated," his friends and pupils continued to visit him, to listen to his talk on philosophy and literature. The book will also tell of the Spanish lawyer, Antonio Amat, who tried to build a coalition of democratic groups, and has been in prison without trial since November, 1958; and of two white men persecuted by their own race for preaching that the coloured races should have equal rights. Ashton Jones, the sixty-five-year-old minister, who last year was repeatedly beaten-up and three times imprisoned in Louisiana and Texas for doing what the Freedom Riders are now doing in Alabama; and Patrick Duncan, the son of a former South African Governor-General, who, after three stays in prison, has just been served with an order forbidding him from attending or addressing any meeting for five years.

'Find out who is in gaol'

The technique of publicising the personal stories of a number of prisoners of contrasting politics is a new one. It has been adopted to avoid the fate of previous amnesty campaigns, which so often have become more concerned with publicising the political views of the imprisoned than with humanitarian purposes.

How can we discover the state of freedom in the world to-day? The American philosopher, John Dewey, once said: "If you want to establish some conception of a society, go find out who is in gaol." This is hard advice to follow, because there are few governments which welcome inquiries about the number of Prisoners of Conscience they hold in prison. But another test of freedom one can apply is whether the Press is allowed to criticise the government. Even many democratic governments are surprisingly sensitive to Press criticism. In France, General de Gaulle has intensified newspaper seizures, a policy he inherited from the Fourth Republic. In Britain and the United States occasional attempts are made to draw the sting of Press criticism by the technique of taking editors into confidence about a "security secret," as in the Blake spy case.

Within the British Commonwealth, the Government of Ceylon has launched an attack on the Press, and is threatening to take the whole industry under public control. In Pakistan the Press is at the mercy of the Martial Law administration. In Ghana, the opposition Press operates under great disabilities. In South Africa, which leaves the Commonwealth on Wednesday, the government is planning further legislation to censor publications. Outside the Commonwealth, Press freedom is especially in peril in Indonesia, the Arab world, and Latin American countries such as Cuba. In the Communist world, and in Spain and Portugal, Press criticism of the Government is rarely tolerated.

Churchill's dictum on democracy

Another test of freedom is whether the government permits a political opposition. The post-war years have seen the spread of "personal régimes" across Asia and Africa. Wherever an opposition party is prevented from putting up candidates, or from verifying the election results, much more than its own future is at stake. Multi-party elections may be cumbrous in practice, and the risk of coalitions makes for unstable government; but no other way has yet been found to guarantee freedom [illegible] Winston Churchill's dictum: "Democracy is a damned bad system of government, but nobody has thought of a better."

A fourth test of freedom is whether [illegible] lawyer is able to present the defence in the way he thinks best. In recent years there has been a regrettable trend in some of those countries that take pride in possessing an independent judiciary: by declaring a state of emergency and taking their opponents into "preventive detention," governments have side-stepped the need to make and prove criminal charges. At the other extreme there is the enthusiasm in Soviet countries to set up institutions which, though called courts, are really nothing of the sort. The so-called "comradely courts" in the U.S.S.R., which have power to deal with "parasites," are in essence little more than departments of the Ministry of Labour, shifting "square pegs" into empty holes in Siberia. In China the transmigration of labour by an allegedly judicial process is on a gigantic scale.

The most rapid way of bringing relief to Prisoners of Conscience is publicity, especially publicity among their fellow-citizens. With the pressure of emergent nationalism and the tensions of the Cold War, there are bound to be situations where governments are led to take emergency measures to protect their existence. It is vital that public opinion should insist that these measures should not be excessive, nor prolonged after the moment of danger. If the emergency is to last a long time, then a government should be induced to allow its opponents out of prison, to seek asylum abroad.

Frontier control more efficient

Although there are no statistics, it is likely that recent years have seen a steady decrease in the number of people reaching asylum. This is not so much due to the unwillingness of other countries to offer shelter, as to the greatly increased efficiency of frontier control, which to-day makes it harder for people to get away. Attempts to reach agreement on a workable international convention on asylum at United Nations have dragged on for many years with little result.

There is also the problem of labour restrictions on immigrants in many countries. So long as work is not available in "host" countries, the right of asylum is largely empty. Appeal for Amnesty, 1961, aims to help towards providing suitable employment for political and religious refugees. It would be good if in each "host" country a central employment office for these people could be set up with the co-operation of the employers' federations, the trade unions and the Ministry of Labour.

In Britain there are many firms willing to give out translation and correspondence work to refugees, but no machinery to link supply with demand. Those régimes that refuse to allow their nationals to seek asylum on the ground that they go abroad only to conspire, might be less reluctant if they knew that, on arrival, the refugees would not be kicking their heels in idle frustration.

The members of the Council of Europe have agreed a Convention of Human Rights, and set up a commission to secure its enforcement. Some countries have accorded to their citizens the right to approach the commission individually. But some, including Britain, have refused to accept the jurisdiction of the commission over individual complaints, and France has refused to ratify the Convention at all. Public opinion should insist on the establishment of effective supra-national machinery not only in Europe but on similar lines in other continents.

This is an especially suitable year for an Amnesty Campaign. It is the centenary of President Lincoln's inauguration, and of the beginning of the Civil War which ended with the liberation of the American slaves; it is also the centenary of the decree that emancipated the Russian serfs. A hundred years ago Mr. Gladstone's budget swept away the oppressive duties on newsprint and so enlarged the range and freedom of the Press. 1861 marked the end of the tyranny of King "Bomba" of Naples, and the creation of a united Italy; it was also the year of the death of Lacordaire, the French Dominican opponent of Bourbon and Orleanist oppression.

The success of the 1961 Amnesty Campaign depends on how sharply and powerfully it is possible to rally public opinion. It depends, too, upon the campaign being all-embracing in its composition, international in character and politically impartial in direction. Any group is welcome to take part which is prepared to condemn persecution regardless of where it occurs, who is responsible or what are the ideas suppressed. How much can be achieved when men and women of good will unite was shown during World Refugee Year. Inevitably most of the action called for by Appeal for Amnesty, 1961, can only be taken by governments. But experience shows that in matters such as these governments are prepared to follow only where public opinion leads. Pressure of opinion a hundred years ago brought about the emancipation of the slaves. It is now for man to insist upon the same freedom for his mind as he has won for his body.

PETER BENENSON

Appeal for Amnesty, 1961

THE AIMS

1. To work impartially for the release of those imprisoned for their opinions.
2. To seek for them a fair and public trial.
3. To enlarge the Right of Asylum and help political refugees to find work.
4. To urge effective international machinery to guarantee freedom of opinion.

To these ends, an office has been set up in London to collect and publish information about Prisoners of Conscience all over the world. The first Press Conference of the campaign will be held to-morrow, where speakers will include three M.P.s, John Foster, Q.C. (Con.), F. Elwyn Jones, Q.C. (Lab.), and Jeremy Thorpe (Lib.).

All offers of help and information should be sent to: Appeal for Amnesty, 1, Mitre Court Buildings, Temple, E.C.4.

2. *THE OBSERVER*, London, May 28, 1961

Birth of AI

Amnesty International grew from Peter Benenson's appeal for the forgotten prisoners publicly announced in *The Observer* newspaper, London, and in *Le Monde*, Paris, on 28 May 1961. Articles in other European newspapers publicized the appeal and Mr Benenson's idea immediately achieved wide international support.

3. International press reaction to *THE OBSERVER* appeal

4. Diana Redhouse and (inset) her Amnesty emblem

5. Every Human Rights Day (December 10) an outsize Amnesty candle is lit at a service in one of London's churches, usually by released prisoners of conscience. Here, a Russian and a Rhodesian are lighting the candle in Westminster Abbey in 1976.

6. Sean MacBride, former Irish Foreign Minister

7. Martin Ennals, AI Secretary General since 1968

8. Torturers' faces: former military policemen in the Athens dock, 1975

9. Major Spyros Moustaklis (left), partially paralyzed by Greek torturers, being escorted to the Athens courtroom as a trial witness

10. Lady Amalia Fleming, Greek-born
widow of Sir Alexander Fleming, the
discoverer of penicillin, speaks on the Greek
radio

11. Dr. Joel Filartiga Speratti who died in
detention in Paraguay

12. His father's drawing of the dead young man's body

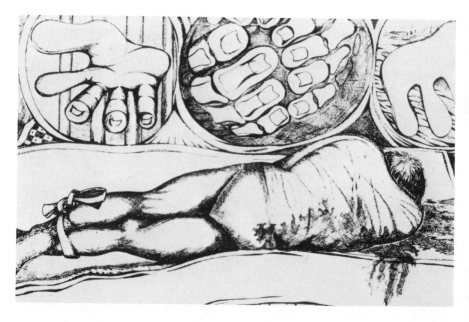

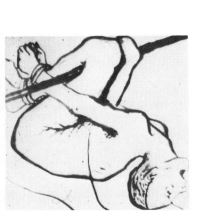

13. An eyewitness' drawing of Brazil's
pau de arara ("parrot's perch") torture
during interrogation
14. Maria Christina Lopez-Stewart, student
of history and geography at the University
of Santiago, 21 years old, disappeared,
presumably killed, in 1974

15. Uruguayan torture of political prisoners

16. Yuri Galanskov, poet

17. Victor Kuznetsov, artist

operating with AI; besides, there were 'no political prisoners in Aden'. Rastgeldi's conclusion was that the whole state of emergency in that former Crown Colony was violating the Declaration of Human Rights. The Foreign Office denied all the charges emphatically and indignantly.

The affair caused a wave of emnity against Amnesty in Britain. The movement was called 'irresponsible'. In Parliament, a Liberal M.P. tried to defend it. There was, he declared, 'a most regrettable failure to deal expeditiou;ly and adequately with the allegations of cruelty', but this did not help to restore Amnesty to official and public favour.

In September, 1966, Peter Benenson decided to go to Aden himself to check Rastgeldi's charges. He returned with sufficient material for a second report which fully supported what Rastgeldi had written. Nothing, said Benenson, fosters suspicion or creates annoyance so much as secretiveness.

What went on behind the scenes of Amnesty's leadership during those days of crisis, as the status of the movement seemed to be endangered, has never been recorded, but one heard that there were 'incipient disagreements'. Peter Archer, in an article on Amnesty in the *Contemporary Review* in 1972, put it into this sentence: 'At the end of 1966, Peter Benenson, whose health had in any event suffered from the intensive work of the last few years, was persuaded that his most effective contribution to the future of Amnesty would be to resign.' The annual Amnesty report stated tersely that Peter Benenson had resigned as President of AI 'over policy differences' in December, 1966.

It must have sounded like the death knell of the movement to the band of loyal supporters who had been with it from the start. Benenson had created it, given it life and shape; many called him the 'Godfather'. How could his creation exist without him? One knew, of course – and the Canterbury meeting two years earlier had brought it already into the limelight – that Benenson and MacBride were no longer seeing eye to eye, but were they not both men who had devoted all their energies to the movement? Was there really no other way of settling differences of opinion within the leadership?

The truth was that Benenson had already begun to withdraw, at least from the less inspiring administrative and other routine jobs, months before his official resignation on the last day of the year. He had to take care of his health, he wanted to enjoy his hobbies – painting and, more recently, farming. He had acquired a farm in Buckinghamshire which he was visiting every few days. It seemed that he was thinking of retiring for good and becoming a 'gentleman farmer'.

His decision was certainly hastened by the acerbating discord with MacBride. Benenson had begun to suspect that secret anti-Amnesty forces were active everywhere — burglars, he said, had stolen documents about Aden from the movement's headquarters, one of its leading officials was working for the British Intelligence Service, the International Commission of Jurists was in the pay of the CIA, and so on. He urged the International Secretariat to move at once to some 'neutral' country — to Sweden, Switzerland, or Luxembourg. MacBride did what he could to heal the rift, and Benenson's resignation at the end of 1966 seems to have been prompted more by his own disappointment with the development of the movement, as he saw it, than by his co-workers' efforts at pushing him out. They were still much too fond of him, and regarded his accusations as the symptoms of a passing brainstorm.

In February, 1967, he held a press conference in his London flat. He charged the British government with suppressing, by censorship, the report — which he had read in a foreign news-paper — that British soldiers had killed fifty Arabs during a demonstration in Aden. He also charged the Labour government with tapping Amnesty's telephone lines.

The Aden story was officially repudiated by the Defence Minister, Denis Healey. The International Executive Committee held a meeting at Elsinore in March, 1967, after the press had made a great splash about Amnesty's 'skeletons in the cupboard' and 'sensational charges', creating the impression that the movement was on its deathbed and the only item to be discussed was the way in which it should be buried.

The meeting, at which Benenson's resignation as President of AI had been discussed, abolished that particular post and created the new one of a Director General instead (later to be modified to Secretary General). The trusted, level-headed, and hard-working Eric Baker was provisionally appointed to it, and he did much to save Amnesty from the fate the press had predicted.

'Early 1967 saw the nadir of Amnesty's fortunes,' recalled Peter Archer. 'Its leadership appeared to be divided, financial disaster threatened, in Britain it was in the position of being simultaneously unpopular with the Foreign Office and accused of being in the pocket of the government, and morale among some groups was low. The crusade of 1961 seemed spent. Yet the work continued by its own momentum, and the majority of groups continued through the long winter to meet in draughty halls, to raise funds, and to write their letters. Between June, 1966, and June, 1967, the number of groups increased from four hundred and ten to five hundred and fifty, and two hundred and ninety-three of the prisoners adopted were released.'

The International Executive, too, was undeterred and prepared its plans for the future. To be sure, during the next few months of 1967, 'Amnesty's staff lived under the perpetual threat that there would shortly be no funds to pay them, but the British section scraped together money from month to month to close the gap. By the end of 1967, the crisis was passed,' wrote Archer, 'Since 1967, Amnesty has continued to expand.'

2

Totalitarian Torture

Behind the Prison Walls: Portugal and Romania
Simultaneously with the report on prison conditions in South
Africa, two further publications on the same subject were issued
by AI in the autumn of 1965, concerning Portugal and Romania.
They dealt with rather different situations. While South Africa
could be likened to a country under foreign occupation, with an
economically powerful, well-armed white minority suppressing a
native black majority and silencing all critics of the system, the
Fascist and Communist dictatorships kept themselves in power
by crushing all opposition among people of their own colour.

Hitler and Stalin were dead and gone, and with them the
period of show trials, of state-organized mass executions and
holocausts which had done immense harm to the names of
Germany and the Soviet Union. Yet the prisons of the totalitarian
states were still full of opponents of these regimes, and Amnesty
had decided to embark on the publication of reports on the
conditions under which such prisoners of conscience were being
held. 'As there are over seventy such countries,' said the fore-
words of the booklets dealing with Portugal and Romania, 'and
all of them by definition conceal what goes on in their prisons,
the undertaking is considerable . . . To execute, torture or incar-
cerate those who commit no other offence than to propound
opinions is to ensure their views a currency and respect they
would not otherwise obtain. In short, political imprisonment is
not only wrong; it is stupid.'

Most of the evidence contained in the reports came from former
prisoners, and there might have been objections to its trustworthi-
ness. But, argued Amnesty, the government in question could

disprove false allegations simply by inviting inspection of prisons by the Red Cross. 'The fact that none of these governments (South Africa, Portugal, Romania) have yet done so speaks for itself.' Another objection might have been that reports such as these would not achieve a great deal in practical terms. This was what the foreword had to say on the matter:

> 'Amnesty International relies upon the power of the *word*. The influence of these reports depends upon the degree of concern of the readers. The men responsible for imprisonment of this character are few in number. Some may read this report themselves and realise that they are inflicting as much needless, outmoded suffering as the surgeon operating without anaesthetic. Others may have their attention drawn to the contents by readers who have been moved to write to them. If the consensus of the decent opinions of mankind has no effect on them, let them reflect soberly that copies of these reports will be on library shelves long after they are dead — and that the supporting evidence by which history will judge them is stored away safely.'

Strong words indeed, reflecting the feeling of revulsion among the Amnesty people at the outrage of locking up men and women merely because they disagree with their governments. This had indeed been the movement's overriding concern during its early years. But these reports on prison conditions brought a new element to the fore. It was the concern not just about the fact that people had been put behind bars, not only about the miserable conditions under which they were being kept, but the systematic use of physical and mental pain that was applied against them behind the prison walls — in short, torture.

The South African report contained a number of statements by ex-prisoners — and also one by a former head warder — telling of violence used in interrogation and as punishment: prisoners were savagely beaten, buried up to their necks in the sand with warders urinating into their mouths, their heads were put into canvas bags, all but suffocating them, whilst they were being hit and kicked, and other primitive forms of torture. The reader got the impression that the men who committed them had been made interrogators or warders by the authorities because of their innate physical and mental brutality, but that the methods they used to intimidate prisoners and extract confessions were left to them. There was, it seemed, no official guidance on prisoners' torture. After all, South Africa in the 1960s was not yet a properly organized dictatorship, nor was, at that time, Rhodesia, which was dealt with in a first Amnesty report published in August, 1966. It told of indiscriminate beatings of prisoners, of threats to castrate them, of electric shocks, of homes wrecked by the police. Again, the forms of brutality and torture were left to the initiative of the policemen, interrogators, and warders. 'It is certain,' said the report, 'that relatively few of the assaults that do take place are ever reported to the proper authorities.' A European priest told Amnesty that 'the police stoutly justified violence, without the slightest attempt to conceal that this was what they were doing. "This is the only language that these people (the blacks) understand . . . We only arrest a man when we know he's guilty . . . If he's not going to tell us the names of those who told him what to do, we've got to beat it out of him."'

In contrast, the report on Portugal showed a fully-fledged totalitarian state in well-organized action. The Portuguese PIDE, the political police under Salazar, were obviously instructed to establish membership of the Communist party with every person they questioned, and the method for extracting that confession especially recommended to them by their superiors was the 'statue' torture. It meant that the prisoner had to stand all the time, often being beaten when he sat or fell down. It also entailed preventing him from sleeping for more than ten minutes at a time, so that eventually he almost or completely lost his reason.

The 'statue' torture was widely used against the students arrested in 1964-65, many of them teenagers. Among them was Maria de Azevedo whose father, after many fruitless attempts, was finally allowed to see her in prison. He was courageous enough to write to the Minister of the Interior, saying that he hardly recognized his daughter: 'Her face was that of a corpse; she could not co-ordinate her ideas and had difficulty in the articulation of words. She could not stand up properly, but walked clutching the walls. All this shows clearly that during her isolation by the PIDE she was subjected to violent treatment, to the torture of no sleep and perhaps to other kinds of violence. And all this was done to a young girl who had never been in trouble with the police . . .'. The writer was summoned to the PIDE and threatened with prosecution 'for spreading false news likely to alarm the public, and for damaging the prestige of the country abroad'.

The trial of thirty-one students in August, 1965, was attended by a British barrister as an observer. He reported that they had all been subjected to the 'statue' treatment, interrogated for up to one hundred and eighty hours without sleep, kept in tiny solitary-confinement cells for up to ten days. As a result, only six of them were able to refuse to sign the confession of 'Communist activities' which the PIDE put before them.

Recalcitrant prisoners were often given some crude psychological treatment to make them confess. Mothers and/or fathers were brought into the interrogation rooms and put under pressure to influence their child, or an older, married student was shown a faked letter saying that his wife had taken up with other men while he was in prison. Sometimes pistols were brandished before prisoners to frighten them, or they were simply told that they would never leave the place alive.

Portugal, a kingdom until 1911, had been an authoritarian state since 1926 when a military junta took over after a period of upheavals and revolutions. A professor of economics at the University of Coimbra, Dr. Oliveira Salazar, was appointed Minister of Finance and rose to the post of Prime Minister in 1932. He succeeded in turning the country into a one-man dictatorship after Mussolini's fashion, devoting more and more of its meagre resources to the upkeep of its vast colonial empire in Africa. No opposition party was allowed to function, civil liberties were largely abolished, dissidents rigorously persecuted. The political police ruled the public and private life of the citizens. During the first twenty-odd years of Salazar's regime, police and justiciary methods were similar to those in Hitler's Germany and Franco's Spain; political prisoners were brutally beaten, and many died as a result. Burning and electric shocks, preferably applied to the sexual organs, were frequently used for extracting confessions.

Compared to these earlier tortures, those reported in the 1960s were slightly less coarse, and the reputedly worst of all Portuguese prisons, the Aljube at Lisbon, was about to be closed. It specialized in torture by isolation, as described by one former inmate: 'I was confined for sixteen days in a concrete cell whose length was that of my body; the width was twice the span of my hands, i.e. less than seventy cms; the height under two metres. There was no light whatsoever in the cell, no window and no ventilation except through three bars at the door. The light outside the cell was switched on only during interrogation; the rest of the time I was in darkness, and I had to eat my food entirely by feeling with my hands.'

There were thirteen solitary-confinement cells in the Aljube prison, and some prisoners spent months and even years in them. They were alone in the darkness, unable to read, and not allowed any exercise at all. Even Lord Russell of Liverpool — the only British outsider invited by the Portuguese government to inspect their prisons, probably because he did not believe the former inmates' allegations — had to admit the utter barbarity of the prisoners' treatment. 'Those who are confined to these tiny cells,' he wrote in his report, 'looked rather like caged animals. I tried to speak to one of them, who was in Cell 13, and he just stared back at me as though he had seen a ghost. There was a coloured youth from Angola in another cell, I think it was No. 16, to whom I spoke. In spite of the fact that my identity was explained to him, he appeared to be terrified when I talked with him through an interpreter, and he shook all over.' What value, one wonders, could a 'confession' by such a prisoner have for the authorities? Neither could the interrogators rely on the validity of the names he might tell them as those of his fellow-conspirators. A man at the end of his strength would say anything to stop his suffering.

When AI published its report on prison conditions in Portugal in 1965, that country was still a dictatorship, but in the case of Romania, the report had only historical value. For in the previous year, the last of the about 12,000 prisoners serving sentences for 'infringements of state security' had been released — the vast majority, if not all, of the country's political prisoners. They had come from a wide range of social and ideological backgrounds: the anti-Communist intelligentsia, the peasants opposed to collectivization, the political parties dissolved in 1947-48, the Orthodox and the Roman Catholic Churches, the pre-war Fascist Iron Guard organization, employees of western embassies and business firms and journalists working for the western press, Zionist Jews, as well as leaders of ethnic minorities such as Serbs, Hungarians, and Turks. Announcing the widest measure of amnesty, the government said that progress in economic and other fields had been so extensive that the Romanian people had become 'united in building Socialism' and those imprisoned for political offences should now be given a chance to work and live normally. Romanian prison conditions had been widely written about in western newspapers, protests and appeals for clemency had been launched by organizations in many countries, but it is difficult to assess the influence it all had on the Romanian government's decision to free its prisoners.

One might argue that Amnesty should not have published its report on Romania's prisons at all at a time when they were already empty of political detainees; that it might have saved its efforts and none-too-abundant funds to appeal for the release of people who were still incarcerated. After all, it would not have been Amnesty's task either to report about Hitler's, Mussolini's or Stalin's atrocities: that was, and still is, a matter for historians, not for campaigners. However, Amnesty's reasons for publishing were: 'First, because the sensible attitude of the Romanian government is not shared by all other Communist countries; in some of them conditions such as those described in Romania a few years back still continue. Second, because it is important to emphasize that, if the Romanian government can afford to take the risk of releasing their political opponents, they should not stop short once the prison gates are unlocked. They should bind up the wounds which they themselves have inflicted, restore the released prisoners to their homes, their social benefits and their jobs.'

Also, some of the Romanian methods of the 1950s, as described in the report, were worth recording if only for their originality. A new prisoner was forced to write his complete autobiography, naming all people with whom he had ever been in contact. When he had finished writing, it was invariably rejected as inadequate by the interrogators and he was sent back to his cell where he was put under pressure to confess his political guilt; until he did so he was deprived of sleep. Many prisoners, men and women, were strung up from the ceiling of their cells like carcasses, hands and feet tied together, and beaten. One woman said that she was stripped and beaten with wet ropes. Sometimes the screams of prisoners were recorded on tape and replayed to other prisoners during interrogations. Tape-recorders were also put in the cells of prisoners who had been given drugs to make them talk in their sleep after long interrogations when the facts they had refused to disclose were near the surface of their minds. When the recordings were later played back to them, this had a devastating effect on the prisoners, and they often broke down completely.

Some women were raped in prison by the guards. This had not happened to a young peasant nun, whose religious order demanded chastity as the main prerequisite for novitiates, but she was given sleeping drugs, and after waking she was made to believe that she had been raped. The shock was so great that she confessed to anything the interrogators wanted to hear.

One method commonly used in Romanian prisons was the

so-called *maneg*. The prisoner was put in a completely empty cell, without even a bed, made to take off all his clothes except his underpants, and then forced to walk barefoot around the cell for six hours at a time; when he slackened he was beaten. In some cases, gravel was thrown on the floor, making every step painful. After a week or so of the *maneg*, few prisoners had any resistance left in them.

Another ingenious torture was the salt diet. Everything the prisoner was given to eat was highly salted, but he got nothing to drink. There were also cases in which the prisoners' teeth were pulled out.

The trial, when it came, was usually no more than a farce. Leonard Kirschen, who had been the Bucharest correspondent of Associated Press, was told by his interrogators: 'Don't think this court is going to try you and decide on your fate. The dossier goes to them with *our* decision. We are the ones who decide on your punishment. The trial is just a formality. If you retract in court what you've told us here, we'll bring you back and take the hide off you.'

Two Missions to Greece
In 1968, Martin Ennals was appointed Secretary General of AI. Born in 1927 as one of three brothers — who all made their way in British public life — he studied international relations and international law and joined UNESCO in Paris in 1950. From 1959 to 1966 he was General Secretary of the National Council of Civil Liberties in Britain and then worked at the National Committee for Commonwealth Immigrants, but he took time off for travelling in Africa to investigate social problems on the spot, especially those of the Asian minorities in East Africa who had opted for British nationality and were in a difficult situation in the newly independent countries. When the British government passed a bill restricting the immigration of these Commonwealth citizens, he resigned and accepted Amnesty's offer of the movement's top post. His appointment opened a new chapter in AI's history.

His first major tasks were the presentation of the movement's new statute, which was to be adopted by the International Assembly in Stockholm in the autumn of 1968, and the reorganizing and strengthening of AI, which was growing again rapidly after overcoming its internal crisis of the mid-1960s. There were now twenty national sections, six hundred and forty groups, and fifteen thousand individual members. Prisoners in seventy-five countries had been adopted, and the budget — now being administered by a new honorary treasurer, the lawyer Anthony Marreco, who was one of the British Counsels at the Nuremberg war criminals' trials — had risen to £23,000. The Stockholm statute streamlined the movement's administration to make it fit for coping with what Ennals called its 'mammoth objective'. The most important result of the Assembly, however, was the inclusion of a new article among its aims, based on Article Five of the Universal Declaration of Human Rights, also embodied in the European Convention of Human Rights: 'No one shall be subjected to torture or to cruel, inhuman or degrading treatment or punishment.'

The Swedish Amnesty section, then the liveliest of all national sections, had prepared the proposal of this new aim at a conference on torture four weeks before the Assembly. The direct cause was the Greek coup of April, 1967, which had brought a right-wing military junta to power. Very soon there were reports of the arrest and ill-treatment of some six thousand people: oppositional politicians, leftist intellectuals, artists, trade unionists, students and journalists. Many were kept in prison only because they refused to sign the Declaration of Loyalty to the new regime.

This regime bore all the characteristic marks of a Fascist dictatorship, with its deliberately created climate of fear. The western world tried, as it had done so often before, to dismiss these reports as 'atrocity stories'. One could not believe that such things were happening in one's beloved Greece, the birthplace of European art and philosophy, the cradle of Occidental democracy.

Amnesty took action at the end of 1967. Anthony Marreco, as a member of the English Bar, and James Becket, a member of the American Bar, went to Athens. Marreco had investigated imprisonment in Paraguay and Rhodesia the year before; Becket spoke Greek and knew the country well. The International Secretariat had asked them to report on two matters: the extent of an amnesty for political prisoners announced by the junta just before Christmas, and the situation of the dependants of those still in prison.

After four weeks of investigations the two lawyers reported that the much-publicised amnesty had not applied to the two thousand seven hundred and seventy-seven people in the prison islands of Leros and Yaros, but only to fewer than three hundred detainees sentenced by court martial after the April coup — and many of them had not been set free at all but merely transferred from one prison camp to another. In addition there were numerous people held without trial in prisons and police stations throughout Greece. Some might have been active Communists, but the remainder 'cannot be described as Communists in the accepted European sense of the word', added the report. 'Large numbers of them are old and infirm, having been arrested on security files prepared in many cases twenty years ago. It seems a feature of the present regime that the government treats such persons as expendable outcasts to be deprived of all political rights.'

Although the lawyers' brief had not included the investigation of torture, this aspect of the junta's regime thrust itself on their attention. What they found out confirmed the worst stories that had made their way to Amnesty in London. The lawyers, though they had to restrict their investigations to Athens, were able to interview sixteen released victims of torture and obtained evidence about thirty-two others who were still in prison. This was no easy achievement, for 'the risk of police interference with Greeks who made contact with an Amnesty representative deterred the majority of victims from doing so, and endangered the few who did', as the lawyers reported. For Greece, torture was a question with far-reaching legal, as well as humanitarian implications, as the country had signed — before the Colonels' junta usurped power — the European Convention of Human Rights banning the use of 'inhuman or degrading treatment'. This provision is one from which no country can derogate, no matter what its domestic situation, while remaining a member of the Council of Europe.

Yet inhuman and degrading treatment was precisely what the junta was meting out to its arrested opponents. Mr. Marreco and Mr. Becket listed twenty-two documented methods of torture, physical and psychological. They reported:

'The standard initial torture . . . is the so-called *falanga*. The prisoner is tied to a bench and the soles of his feet are beaten with a stick or pipe. Between beatings the prisoner is usually made to run around the bench under a heavy rain of blows. One prisoner now in Averoff prison had his foot broken under this torture. As he went without medical attention, the bones have not set properly and he is crippled.' Other evidence proved that sexually-oriented torture had been used, psychological pressure applied, electric shocks given for lengthy periods. Prisoners were struck on the breastbone and vomited blood as a result; when they screamed with pain from the *falanga*, water was poured down their mouths and noses, or soap powder was put in their eyes, mouths, and noses. Sometimes their throats were grasped in such a way that their windpipes were cut off; filthy rags, often soaked in urine, were shoved down their throats. Their naked flesh was beaten with wires knotted together into a whip. Warders jumped on their stomachs. Pepper was rubbed on the genitals, eyes, noses and other sensitive parts of the body; burning cigarettes were put out on their skins. Generally, from four to six men were beating prisoners with their fists, with planks, pipes, canes and so on or kicked with booted feet. At one camp, which housed Greece's *élite* soldiers, prisoners were made to run a gauntlet; one prisoner had 'literally his eye knocked out of his head'.

The Marreco-Becket report was issued by Amnesty in January, 1968, and received widespread press, radio, and television publicity. The Greek rulers must have become rather embarrassed and nervous: after all, such stories were bound to harm tourism, the country's major source of income. So they invited Mr. Marreco again to continue his investigation with official cooperation, to prove to the world that Amnesty's allegations were unfounded. Marreco accepted.

This time, twelve prisoners were produced by the authorities, and Marreco interviewed them in the presence of police and prison officials. Nine of them had the guts to say they had been tortured, and one said he would rather not answer the question. Mr. Marreco gave the nine names to Mr. Pattakos, Deputy Prime Minister and Minister of the Interior, and requested an immediate public inquiry into the matter, with criminal charges against the officials named as torturers by the prisoners. Mr. Pattakos refused categorically — because all the prisoners were 'known Communists'. In fact, Marreco knew that in one case at least this was a blatant lie: the man was a leading member of the Centre Union Party and a sociologist of international repute. But even if the rest had been Communists, Greece had violated the Human Rights Convention.

The three Scandinavian countries Sweden, Norway, and Denmark had already put the case against the Greek junta before the European Commission on Human Rights in Strasbourg in 1967, charging them with breaking eight Convention articles. Now, after publication of the two Amnesty reports, the Scandinavians amended their complaints to include the violation of a ninth article, that on torture. Then followed the Swedish Amnesty conference on torture, already mentioned, and the International

Assembly at Stockholm in the autumn of 1968, which decided to include the relevant Human Rights article in the statute of Amnesty International.

Meanwhile, the charges against the Greek government intensified. A sub-commission of the European Commission of Human Rights gathered more evidence, which was published in a four-volume report. The junta, desperately trying to wriggle out of its tight corner, started intense diplomatic activity to avoid Greece's humilating expulsion from the Council of Europe, going as far as promising free elections and the 'restoration of democracy'. It was too late. There was a dramatic session of the Council of Europe; the Greek delegation tried to defend its position, and the Foreign Minister made an eloquent speech. But the vast majority of the Council was clearly against him, and under orders from Athens he walked out before the vote on expulsion was passed.

It was a great vindication of Amnesty International as a guardian of human rights, but it was only a moral victory. Injustice and torture continued in Greece, with the military police taking the lead until the junta was ousted in July, 1974, and a civilian government took its place.

The Torturers' Trial

A year later, in August, 1975, the first batch of torturers — fourteen officers and eighteen NCOs — were brought to trial before the Athens Court Martial on charges of torture. They were all members of the ESA, the junta's military police which had been endowed with nearly absolute powers of arrest, interrogation, and detention in 1968. Amnesty published the proceedings and their background in a hundred-page booklet, *Torture in Greece.* It showed that all that had been said in the first Amnesty reports had been true, and if they had erred it was only on the count of underrating the extent and ferocity of prisoners' maltreatment.

'At the outset of the ESA torture routine,' said the trial report, 'prisoners would be deprived of both food and drink. They would be told to remain standing in the corner of their cell, sometimes on one foot but usually at attention. This ordeal would last for several days. It would often be interspersed with beating — standings and beatings together known as a "tea party with toast". If the prisoner fell down, he would be made to resume his standing position . . . After standing upright for a few days and being deprived of refreshment, the victim would normally begin to

46

experience hallucinations . . . A United States citizen who was arrested in 1970 said: "I began to see that I had two faces, one in front and one behind. I was delirious. I began to insult the government and everyone there . . . Then I tried to separate my soul from my body so that I could leave my body to be tortured.'"

A lawyer imagined under this torture that he saw a refrigerator on the wall, and said to the guard, 'Why don't you open it and give me a Coca Cola?' Eventually, the prisoner would be given some food and drink, but sometimes the water would contain soap or salt to increase the thirst. 'I had hallucinations from thirst and standing upright,' said a former Lieutenant-General who had been arrested. 'At one moment my cell was left open. I tried to escape. I ran in the direction of the U.S. Embassy, but they caught up with me. Then they beat me for two hours . . . I woke up in a cell and my feet were swollen. Blood and liquid were running from my wounds, and I had a terrible pain in my chest. I wanted to kill myself . . . Sometimes I drank my own urine.'

Many prisoners wanted to commit suicide. One, a law student, told the court: 'Kainich (an interrogator) beat me daily. Before beating me, he would sadistically show me the size of his fist and a monogrammed ring which he wore and which made his blows much more painful. I began to cough up blood . . . I was the sandbag and he was the boxer . . . One morning he threw me into a pile of bricks and began to hit me with them and kick me, preferably in the genitals. That day I decided to kill myself . . . The worst torture was waiting to be tortured . . . I was obsessed with the idea of suicide. But I suddenly came to my senses and rejected the idea. I thought my death would only help the dictatorship. I swore an oath — I am coming out of here alive. I shall live, it is my duty to live.'

At one point in the trial proceedings the prosecuting major asked, 'How could Greek officers sink to this moral degradation? Were they born with criminal instincts, or did external circumstances deform their characters? It is certain that those morally responsible are not in this court. They are those who used the defendants, who inspired in them wrong ideas about our national interest. They are those who, for many years, have given thousands of hours of instruction on the fight against Communism, without devoting even one hour to the defence of democracy.'

The officers in the dock were unrepentant and tried to keep their subordinate soldiers from telling the truth, but without much success. 'We served under them,' said one soldier, 'and now they haven't the courage to take responsibility for what they ordered.' Another soldier said, 'Our reward (for obedience) was to be ruined and get a bad name which will stick throughout our lives; to carry out their crazy ideas. They ought to have killed themselves. Instead, they try to throw the blame on us.' Again, as in the Nuremberg trials, the subordinate men claimed that they were 'only obeying orders', while their superiors denied having instructed them to use torture. The court, however, did not accept these pleas.

Some glimpses of the mentality of the accused emerged during the testimonies of the victims. There were strong implications of sexual perversities, not just obscene language and threats of castration, which were fairly common, but also some very odd symptoms of the torturers' warped libidos. 'I don't think Kainich is normal,' said the student we have quoted above. 'When he had beaten us in turn in the cells, he would go out into the corridor and order us to lie on our beds and act as if we were having intercourse with a woman. Then he would shout, "And I want to hear noises!"' Another interrogator exposed his sexual organ to a prisoner and threatened to violate him. Alexandros Panagoulis, whom the trial report called 'probably the most sexually abused prisoner', was seized by the genitals by an officer when he was brought in; the same officer later surpervised the insertion of an iron needle up that prisoner's urinary tract. Another officer showed ex-Commander Apostolos, also a prisoner, a photograph of a naked man and woman, covering their heads, and hinted that the woman was the Commander's wife with another man, boasting that the ESA was able to take telescopic photographs at night. He showed other prisoners photographs of naked women, alleging that they were their girl friends.

'It is important to see that these individual perversions are not the cause of a system of torture,' explained the report. 'Rather, once a system of torture has been created in order to support the political needs of those in power, the rulers' agents will exhibit patterns of behaviour that they would not otherwise be in a position to do.' Or, in simpler terms: torturers with perverted minds find in defenceless prisoners the ideal objects for acting out their sexual fantasies. One might ask whether such a perverted mind is not the basic characteristic that makes a man a good torturer.

Odd behaviour, to judge by the witnesses' evidence, seems to have been the rule rather than the exception among the investigators and guards. One prisoner, also a lawyer, was pelted by officers and soldiers with maccaroni and mince in the canteen — probably as a kind of joke. He had to relieve himself in front of an armed guard and others who mocked him. An imprisoned former Wing Commander was told by the interrogating officer 'in a quiet and gentle tone': 'You know, we have the means of making anyone confess anything. You know, it is possible that some parts of your body might be destroyed.' Later he was told that his wife and child had also been arrested. 'What you and they are going to suffer!' said the interrogator and put on a tape recording of his wife 'weeping and beseeching'.

Lady Amalia Fleming, the Greek-born widow of Sir Alexander Fleming, the discoverer of penicillin, was arrested on a visit to her native country, where she was known as an opponent of the junta. 'They called me a Communist,' she told the court. 'I wanted to vomit. This thrilled them. You must know that humiliation is one of their main aims. The vomiting was a means of torture. They smeared people with their own vomit. They put a desk in front of me and began to rock it whilst others opened and shut the drawers in order to make me feel seasick. I tried to steady myself with my hands. I don't know how long it lasted . . . They told me they would torture others in front of me and would tell them they were being tortured because I would not speak and give the names they were asking for. This nearly drove me mad.'

Lady Fleming's treatment showed the confusion of the torturers' minds, or perhaps of the instructions they got from their superiors. One minute she would be warned, 'I will pull your teeth out, one by one!', the next minute she would be offered a ministry — this happened, in fact, three times. When the investigators saw that she needed water, they made her wait for it for twenty hours. She suffered a severe haemorrhage. The prison doctor came and revealed to her that he had orders to keep her in good condition.

Numerous women prisoners were subjected to sexual assaults. The torturers shoved as many fingers as possible, or an object, into the vagina and twisted and tore brutally. Tubes were inserted into the anus and water driven into the prisoner at very high pressure. Hair was pulled out from the head and pubic regions.

Many of these forms of torture had already been listed in the Marreco-Becket report and were now confirmed before the court. One must not forget that this report was compiled during the first few months of the junta's regime; six and a half years of it were still to come, years of Amnesty's intensive work for Greece's political prisoners and of appeals to the world's conscience. Again, one might ask, why revive the memory of an era which, as all friends of that country hope, has gone for ever? Here the answer is obvious. 'Foremost in our minds,' said the preface of Amnesty's trial report, 'was the need to present the essence of this historic trial to the non-Greek world as a welcome example of submitting accused torturers to due process of law,' an example which should be understood as a warning to the torturers and their instigators in other dictatorial regimes. Amnesty also drew particular attention to two relevant 'Nuremberg Principles', or guidelines at the war criminals' trials, for bringing to justice those responsible for prisoners' custody but who violated those prisoners' basic human rights: 'The fact that a person acted as Head of State or as responsible government official does not relieve him of responsibility for committing any of the offences defined in this (the International Law) code', and 'the fact that a person charged with an offence defined in this code acted pursuant to an order of his government or of a superior does not relieve him of responsibility in international law if, in the circumstances at the time, it was possible for him not to comply with that order.'

A no less relevant question was put to the judges by the father of one of the accused soldiers at the Athens trial: 'We are a poor but decent family,' said the father, a farmer, 'and now I see him in the dock as a torturer. I want to ask the court to examine how a boy who everyone said was "a diamond" became a torturer, who morally destroyed my family and my home?'

Chile after Allende

In December, 1972, Amnesty International began a world-wide 'Campaign for the Abolition of Torture', CAT for short. Sean MacBride, then Chairman of Amnesty's International Executive Committee, opened it with these words: 'The growth of torture has been described as epidemic. To control dissent and maintain power, governments have submitted torture to intellectual analyses and produced progressively more sophisticated methods of cowing, punishing, and eliminating real or imagined opponents of their regimes.'

The following year, the U.N. General Assembly approved of an Amnesty-inspired resolution formally denouncing torture. It called on all governments to 'adhere to existing international instruments forbidding the practice of torture'. A strong incentive had been that representatives of 110,000 policemen in Belgium, Denmark,

Finland, France, Norway and Sweden had signed the CAT appeal to the United Nations for creating an effective machinery to outlaw torture. At the end of the year, an international conference in Paris discussed ways and means of putting the resolution into practice. Early in 1973, Amnesty published the first edition of an international survey on torture during the preceding ten years (a second edition, brought up to date, was published in 1975).

It is a terrible document. No fewer than sixty countries were here indicted; but it may have surprised many readers that the Communist countries got off comparatively lightly in the report. There were certain reasons for that. 'Since the death of Stalin,' it said, 'attitudes towards torture have considerably changed in Eastern Europe and the Soviet Union. Until then, the use of torture had been condoned and encouraged in Russia and also in countries of Eastern Europe. Indeed, one of the few extant directives from a national authority on the use of torture came from Stalin. His Central Committee circular telegram in code to the NKVD organization of January 20, 1939, formally confirmed the use of torture.'

It was revealed by Khrushchev in his famous 'secret speech' to the Party Congress in 1956; this is what the telegram said:

'The Party Central Committee explains that application of methods of physical pressure in NKVD practice is permissable from 1937 on . . . It is known that all bourgeois intelligence services use methods of physical influence against the representatives of the Socialist proletariat and that they use them in the most scandalous forms. The question arises as to why the Socialist intelligence service should be more humanitarian against the mad agents of the bourgeoisie, against the deadly enemies of the working class and of the collective farm workers. The Party Central Committee considers that physical pressure should still be used obligatorily, as an exception applicable to known and obstinate enemies of the people, as a method both justifiable and appropriate.'

Khrushchev's speech with its revelations of Stalin's terror marked a watershed. Torture as a government-sanctioned practice had ceased, stated the report: 'With a few exceptions, no reports on the use of torture in Eastern Europe have been reaching the outside world in the past decade . . . It should, however, be added that the Communist government has always placed a higher priority on economic advancement than on the protection of the rights of the individual.'

An article in the American journal *TIME*, however, had a somewhat more blunt explanation (August, 1976): 'In many Communist nations this (torture) is simply not necessary: the torture chamber, anti-Communists argue, is countrywide. All-powerful, vigilant party apparatus, supported by huge secret police forces, make opposition almost impossible; thus torture on a grand scale is superfluous.' Labour camps for 're-educating' dissidents, the article added, can produce agony bordering on torture, and then there is the time-honoured Russian method of locking dissidents up in mental hospitals, with low-calorie diets and drug treatment, under the pretence that anyone finding fault with such a splendid social and political system must be mad.

The Amnesty world survey of torture, therefore, may have looked somewhat one-sided with its emphasis on Africa, Central and South America, the Middle East, and Asia. But there was indeed plenty to report. The evidence collected by Amnesty — though admittedly representing 'only a small part of the practice of torture' — was shockingly abundant. The then latest reports came from Chile, where in September, 1973, the constitutionally elected government of President Salvador Allende had been overthrown by a swift but extremely violent military coup. Allende himself was killed. Within a few weeks, an Amnesty delegation went to that country to investigate the flood of allegations of torture and maltreatment. This was what the delegation reported:

'In an atmosphere of extreme xenophobia, many thousands of foreign refugees and visitors were imprisoned or expelled; thousands of Chilean civilians lost their lives, either killed during the brief fighting, or executed without trial or after drum-head courts martial within hours of their arrest. An estimated 40,000 Chileans* were detained, denounced by neighbours or professional associates, or arrested by the military merely because of the positions they held during the previous government. All pro-Allende newspapers, magazines, radios and other media were closed down; their directors were killed, imprisoned or forced to seek asylum. All political parties that had formed the Popular Unity coalition of the Allende government were outlawed; leaders and militants of these parties were subjected to immediate and bitter persecution. The Central Workers' Union was immediately declared illegal, and the right to strike and the right to freedom of association were terminated. The military immediately assumed administrative powers over the universities and hospitals. Recognised Allende supporters among teachers and students were expelled from the universities, a vast number being detained. A State of War was declared on September 22nd, drastically limiting civilian freedoms and permitting

*Total population of Chile: 8½ million.

52

the military to arrest, interrogate, detain and judge whomsoever it wishes for as long as it wishes. . .

'Torture has been common practice during the interrogation of political prisoners; confessions extracted by torture have been considered as admissible evidence by the military tribunals. This widespread use of torture has been documented by a number of international organizations that have carried out investigations in Chile since the coup, as well as by foreign diplomats, journalists and lawyers who have observed trials, leading members of the Chilean church, the relatives of political prisoners and (naturally) the ex-prisoners themselves. . .

'In the first weeks after the coup, no fewer than 45,000 people were detained for political reasons. During interrogation, the majority of prisoners were kicked, beaten, threatened, and subjected to many kinds of physical and moral pressures. . . Many were killed, others were forced to stand naked for hours while being continuously beaten with rifle butts. . The purpose of such brutality appears to have been intimidation, rather than any genuine attempt to extract confessions on which to base criminal charges.

'Though not *all* prisoners were tortured, all ran the risk of being tortured and were well aware that they had no form of judicial protection during interrogation. Within a few weeks of the coup, prisoners began to be transferred from the larger detention centres to military centres and schools — sixteen of whose names are known to Amnesty International which were specifically equipped for torture. . . Many people were tortured to death by means of endless whipping as well as beating with fists, feet and rifle butts. Prisoners were beaten on all parts of the body, including the head and sexual organs. The bodies of prisoners were found in the Rio Mapocho, sometimes disfigured beyond recognition. Two well-known cases in Santiago are those of Litre Quiroga, the ex-director of prisons under the Allende government, and Victor Jara, Chile's most popular folk-singer. Both were detained in the Estadio Chile and died as a result of torture received there. According to a recurrent report, the body of Victor Jara was found outside the Estadio Chile, his hands broken and his body badly mutilated. Litre Quiroga had been kicked and beaten in front of other prisoners for approximately forty hours before he was moved to a special interrogation room where he met his death under unknown circumstances.

'In other prisons techniques were similar, the degree of brutality depending on the whims of the individual camp commander. There were many cases of burning (with acid or cigarettes), of electricity, of psychological threats including simulated executions and threats that the families of the prisoners would be tortured. At times the brutality reached animalistic levels. Prisoners have been forced to witness or participate in sexual depravities. An unknown number of women have been raped; some of them, pregnant after rape, have been refused abortions. Women have insects forced up their vaginas; pregnant women have been beaten

rifle butts until they have aborted. Prisoners have been forced to eat excrement, have been plunged endlessly into ice-cold water, have had their bones smashed, have been left to stand naked in the sun for many hours. On the boat *Esmeralda,* anchored off the shore at Valparaiso, prisoners were allegedly left naked and tied to the masts of the boat. At times, prisoners were forced to witness the torture and death of others. . .

'In recent months the methods of torture have tended to become more uniform. All prisoners have been hooded during interrogation, both to hide the identity of the torturer and to increase the psychological fears of the prisoner. Psychological torture appears to have become more prominent. Prisoners have been threatened that they would be thrown from windows if they did not make the required confessions. They have been subjected to screams in adjacent cells (either genuine sounds of torture or simulated noises to produce the effect of torture). . . On December 19 one prisoner was found dead, his testicles burned off. . . In *Tejas Verdes* a pregnant woman had electricity applied to her genitals; a prisoner died after his legs had been broken and his genital organs had been burned. . .

'Torture. . . continues, and the judicial process provides no safeguards for the victims. This last fact is clear from the report of Dr. Horst Woesner, Judge of the Federal Court of West Germany, who observed the Air Force trials on behalf of Amnesty International in May, 1974. He reported that when a defence lawyer alleged that his client had been tortured, the court ruled that such allegations constituted political arguments and were therefore inadmissible.'

Brazilian Inventions

Military coups have been the *sine qua non* in Latin American politics ever since the continent's liberation from the Spanish and Portuguese a century and a half ago. Brazil had its latest in March, 1964, and shortly after Amnesty received countless reports of torture of political prisoners, which escalated four years later after a 'sub-coup' had brought a new set of generals and colonels to power. They did away with the last remnants of civil liberties in Brazil.

It is South America's largest country, with a population of almost a hundred million, nominally sixty per cent of them white, the rest blacks, 'mulattos', and a sprinkling of native Indians, but these distinctions are arbitrary as this is a multi-racial society with ethnic elements from many parts of the world. There is no colour prejudice; however, it does seem that Brazilians are generally the poorer the darker their skins, and the vast urban slums of the large cities with their predominantly black population are a constant social challenge to the rulers and a potential source of political unrest. This may explain the tendency of the upper clases in recent times to entrust the country's fortunes to the military strongmen.

In 1970, Amnesty people went to the Brazilian Embassy in London, suggesting that an independent mission to Brazil could serve to improve the country's image abroad if the torture charges proved to be inaccurate. The Embassy's reaction was somewhat sour; the mission was never approved, nor did Amnesty receive any information promised by the Embassy about alleged cases of torture. Amnesty released a press statement on the Brazilian situation. There was a public outcry, yet reports of continued ill-treatment 'of an extremely alarming nature' kept coming in from many sources. Again, Amnesty approached the Embassy about a mission, with the argument that such an investigation 'could not but add to the stature of the Brazilian nation which had played a leading role in the work which culminated in the Inter-American Convention on Human Rights'. Again, the Brazilians refused to receive an Amnesty mission, though the Ambassador wrote that his government had 'a deep and abiding respect for human rights' and was opposed to torture. But these were 'matters of Brazil's internal jurisdiction'.

Meanwhile, Amnesty's dossier on torture in Brazil was growing day by day. Sympathizers had paid unofficial visits to that country and reported what they had found out; testimonies and statements were being issued by a great number of international and church organizations, such as the International Commission of Jurists, the Brazilian Council of Bishops, the Organization of American States (OAS). So, in 1972, Amnesty decided to go ahead and publish a 90-page document on allegations of torture in Brazil, with an appendix — in English, Portuguese, and French — giving the names of one thousand and eighty-one men and women reported to have been tortured, plus a list of four hundred and seventy-two alleged torturers. Before publication the document was submitted to the Brazilian government; its only response was a new press law forbidding the publication of any Amnesty statements on Brazil. No move was made by the government to start an enquiry into the allegations.

'Vera Silva Magalhaes was a twenty-four year old student in Rio de Janeiro when she was arrested by the military police in March, 1970, for "distributing leaflets",' ran one of the case histories. 'Miss Magalhaes says she was suspended for more than seven hours on the notorious *pau de arara* (i.e. the "parrot's perch" — the prisoner's wrists and ankles are tied together and he is suspended from an iron bar under his knees, leaving his naked body doubled over and upside down). She was given repeated electric shocks during the seven hours, water was forced into her mouth and nose, she was beaten with a truncheon and whip all over her body, including her genital area. Her legs became paralyzed.

'Miss Magalhaes was tried and released three months after her arrest. But her case was an exception: generally the detained person is not brought before a judge until he has served approximately one year's detention.'

The *pau de arara* was an original Brazilian invention, but not the only one. There was — or still is — an advanced school of torture, the *Operacao Bandeirantes,* OB for short, at Sao Paulo, run by the 2nd Army, where old and new methods of torture are taught and tried out. Among the refined Brazilian inventions is this one: the end of a reed is placed in the anus of a naked man suspended on the *pau de arara,* and a piece of cotton soaked in petrol is lit at the other end of the reed; pregnant women have been forced to witness this torture of their husbands. Other wives have been hung naked beside their hubands and given electric shocks on the sexual parts of their bodies while subjected to the worst kind of obscenities. Children have been tortured daily before their parents and *vice versa.*

For one pair of young people in Sao Paulo, who had just started what they hoped would be a long friendship, perhaps a lifelong one, a harmless appointment for dinner in 1970 turned out to be the beginning of an agonising tragedy. They were Marcos Arruda, a geologist, son of an American mother, who was on his way to meet Marlene Soccas, a dentist and painter. What he did not know was that she had been arrested as a member of a political organization, taken to *Operacao Bandeirantes,* and brutally tortured. Marcos was picked up by four armed policemen before he reached the meeting place, and was also taken to the OB headquarters. After some initial beating and kicking he had to strip and was given the *pau de arara* torture, with some refinements. A wire was fixed to his little toe and his testicles, with the other end attached to an old-fashioned camp telephone. By turning its handle, the current could be increased or decreased. During this shock treatment he was violently beaten with a *palmatoria,* a board with holes, which produces large haematomes on the victim's body. The torture continued for several hours. Each time he fainted, water was thrown over him to increase the impact of the electric shocks, which were later applied to his eyes, ears, mouth, and nostrils. Six men were busy on the job.

Marcos Arruda gave this description of his torture at the beginning of a long letter to the Pope after he had been released. His ordeal went on though he had no connection whatsoever with his girl-friend's political organization. The letter went on for several pages with a detailed account of all the horrible sufferings at the hands of his torturers. He landed at the military hospital of Sao Paulo where they gave him two hours to live; a padre was called to hear his confession. But when he began to recover, two police-men came and said, 'Now that you are alone we are going to get rid of you. You are going to die,' and beat him up in bed. After six weeks at the hospital he was taken back to OB, tortured again, and again sent to hospital until his trial at which he was acquitted — thanks, it was said, to his family connections abroad.

Meanwhile, Marlene Soccas had also been in the torturers' hands at OB and in other prisons. Two years after her arrest, still awaiting her trial, she wrote to the 'auditor judge' of the Military Tribunal of what had happened to her:

'Brutally stripped by policemen I was put on the "dragon chair" (a kind of metallic plate) with my hands tied to electric wires and various parts of my body, including the tongue, ears, eyes, wrists, breasts, and sex organs. .

I was beaten about the kidneys and the vertebral column; I was burnt with cigarettes, I was tortured in the presence of naked political detainees, men and women. . .

'One of the torturers, an army captain, said to me: "Get ready to see Frankenstein come in!" I saw a man come into the room, walking slowly and hesitantly, leaning on a stick, one eyelid half closed, his mouth twisted, unable to form words, his stomach muscles twitching continuously. He had been admitted to hospital between life and death after traumatic experiences undergone during violent torture. They said to me, "Encourage him to talk; if not, the *Gestapo* will have no more patience and we will kill him, and the responsibility for his death will lie with you.". . .

'I am a painter and when I was arrested, the police took eighteen paintings. . . None have yet been returned to me. What words can one use to describe such actions?

'One day, crossing the courtyard on the men's side, I witnessed a sad spectacle which would not have been allowed even in a Nazi concentration camp: three *correcionais* detainees were thrown into a well with the water reaching to shoulder level; they were surrounded by the military police and jailers with clubs and sticks in their hands. They kept the heads of the three men under water with their feet; it was winter and the unfortunate victims were trembling convulsively, eyes wide open, staring, fixed, appealing, their faces skeletal due to the freezing water. . .'

Marlene Soccas' letter to the judge ended with these pathetic words:

'I have reported here, your Honour, the experiences I have undergone. They are not relevant just for me but for the millions of people who have followed the same path. When I was a young girl, I was taught to love Brazil, to respect its flag, to do my best for its people, to dedicate to my country my brains, my work and, if necessary, my life. These feelings have not changed, the small girl is still inside me, but I know that the illusions died an abrupt death when I was tortured under Brazil's flag. . .

'The world is changing daily. I am not the person who will make it change any quicker, nor can I prevent it from changing, because it is whole peoples who make history. Nothing will prevent the people, once they learn of their lot, from taking into their own hands the control of their destiny and construct a world of justice and solidarity. Even death will not prevent this because those who die for the ideals of justice become symbols of a new life and serve as an inspiration for others to continue the struggle.'

At the time when the Amnesty report on allegations of torture in Brazil was published (1972), Marlene Soccas was still in prison.

Torture in Turkey

Brazil's neighbour, Paraguay, was being ruled under a state of siege by President Alfredo Stroessner, the general who had come to power in 1954 and was re-elected several times. His emergency decrees were officially described as necessary because of a continuing Communist threat. In 1966, AI published a report by its investigator. Torture, 'often resulting in the death of the prisoners concerned,' he wrote, 'is carried on in the presence of top Paraguayan police officials . . . The conditions in which the political prisoners are held are appalling. They are much worse than the conditions of imprisonment of ordinary convicts. In the heat of the Paraguayan summer, a dozen men or more have been kept for months in one humid, dark, and totally inadequate cell. In another cell, three men have been kept in medieval stocks. Torture and beating have been the rule rather than the exception in police interrogations. . . The most disturbing aspect of the present situation is the almost total disregard of the Constitution and the courts by the present government. . .'

American aid, noted the investigator, has given the government in Paraguay an excuse to cry 'Communist' whenever it suits them. If there still was a serious Communist movement it would be 'dormant and dispirited' after most of the leaders had been hunted down and eliminated. This was done by Stroessner's Special Intelligence Department, whose chief had been sent to the U.S. to be trained by the FBI for his job. In a country where capital punishment for criminals is virtually unknown, the killing of six members of a Communist youth organization in 1965 left a deep trauma, a massacre 'all the more horrible in contrast to the natural tolerance and humanity of the Paraguayan people', as the Amnesty report put it. The six had been tortured to death in a police station in Asuncion. The bodies of men who had obviously been tortured to death were fished out of rivers. 'Torture is frequently witnessed by army generals and by a prominent public figure,' said the AI report, 'and is carried out by teams whose members include the mentally deficient and the sexually disturbed.'

Among students in Paraguay, the U.S. and Britain, the case of Professor Luis Resck — adopted by Amnesty as a prisoner of conscience — caused considerable anger. He was a Christian Democrat and had been President of the Students' Union. Between 1957 and 1961 he was arrested, interrogated, beaten and ill-treated no less than thirty-six times; only once was he brought before a court which released him immediately. The thirty-seventh time, however, was during a students' demonstration at which the Professor was to speak on the occasion of Paraguay's 150th anniversary of independence. He was held, without charge, for more than six weeks at police headquarters, and so brutally tortured that he had to be taken to a hospital, from where he was released. During his imprisonment, Mr. Adlai Stevenson happened to visit Paraguay as personal representative of President Kennedy, and the Students' Union handed him a letter pointing out that American aid should be given only to free men and free governments, and that Paraguay did not fulfil these conditions. As a result, Professor Resck was again arrested and tortured, along with half a dozen other professors and students.

'It is characteristic of police methods in Asuncion,' wrote the AI investigator in 1966, 'that having tortured prisoners, the police did not hold them long enough for public opinion to be mobilised. Lesser known political prisoners have not been so fortunate. . . There is no doubt that Professor Resck is of the stuff of martyrs.'

On the other side of the globe, in Turkey, the AI representative Muir Hunter, an eminent English lawyer, came early in 1972 to the conclusion: 'There appears to be a strong *prima facie* case for investigating the allegations of torture, brutality and threats in the treatment of prisoners.' Later in the same year, Hunter returned to Turkey as the leader of an AI mission to investigate the allegations. The Turkish government — after it had categorically declared that 'no ill-treatment whatsoever is inflicted during the questioning' of prisoners, and that there were no 'chambers of torture' to be investigated as they did not exist — invited the mission to visit prisons and talk to prisoners and defence lawyers.

In fact, the authorities allowed the mission 'to interview a single prisoner, a medical student who had attended to the wounds of others, including her husband who, she alleged, had been tortured. Yet the mission succeeded in collecting a mass of authentic material on torture carried out on a large scale, the most common technique being the beating on the soles of the feet with hard rods. 'A strain of sexual sadism in the torturers,' said the mission's report, 'is also evident from the numerous allegations that truncheons and electric prods were inserted into the anuses and vaginas of victims.'

Perhaps the most significant document was the statement of Ayse Semra Eker, a twenty-three year old woman who was seized in the street by several men in 1972. She heard that they were addressing each other as 'colonel' and 'major'. She was blindfolded and forced into a minibus. Her statement continues:

'They started asking me question from the first moment . . . When I did not answer, they started threatening me in the following manner: "You don't talk now," they would say, "in a few minutes, when our hands will start roaming between your legs, you will be singing like a nightingale.". . . I was then taken into the basement of a building before which we had stopped . . . They asked me questions and kept on saying that unless I spoke it would be quite bad for me and that we would have to do "collective training" together. After a short while they forced me to take off my skirt and stockings and laid me down on the ground and beat the soles of my feet for about half an hour. . . They attached wires to my fingers and toes and passed electric current through my body. At the same time they kept beating my naked thighs with truncheons. . . .

'During the tortures, a grey-haired, stout and elderly colonel and a grey-haired, blue-eyed, tall and well-built officer would frequently come in and give directives. After a while, they disconnected the wire from my finger and connected it to my ear. They immediately gave a high dose of electricity. My whole body and head shook in a terrible way. My front teeth started breaking. At the same time my torturers would hold a mirror to my face and say: "Look what is happening to your lovely green eyes. Soon you will not be able to see at all. You will lose your mind . . ." They lifted me up to my feet and . . . started beating me with truncheons. After a while I felt dizzy and could not see very well. Then I fainted. When I came to myself, I found I was lying half-naked in a pool of dirty water. They tried to force me to stand up and run . . . beating me with truncheons, kicking me and pushing me against the walls. They then held my hands and hit me with truncheons, kicking me and pushing me against the walls. They then held my hands and hit me with truncheons on my palms and hands, taking turns. After all this my whole body was swollen and red and I could not stand on my feet. As if all this was not enough, Umit Erdal (one of the torturers) attacked me and forced me to the ground. I fell on my face. He stood on my back and with the assistance of somebody else forced a truncheon into my anus. As I struggled to stand he kept on saying, "You whore! See what else we will do to you. First tell us how many people did you go to bed with? You won't be able to do it any more. We shall next destroy your womanhood" . . . They tried to penetrate my feminine organ with the truncheon. As I resisted they hit my body and legs with a large axe handle. They soon succeeded in pene-trating my sexual organ with the truncheon with the electric wire on it, and passed current. I fainted. A little later, the soldiers outside brought in a machine used for pumping air into people and said they would kill me. Then they untied me, brought me to my feet and took me out of the room. With a leather strap they hanged me from my wrists on to a pipe in a corridor. As I hung half-naked several people beat me with truncheons. I fainted again. . .'

They showed Ayse Eker another badly injured prisoner to frighten her even more; the nails of the right hand had been burnt off, one foot-sole was completely black and ruptured. Both prisoners were taken to Istanbul, where Ayse Eker was further tortured by the MIT, the Turkish Secret Service. She could not eat because her hands were tied to chains — besides, her tongue was split. After ten days she was sent to a 'house of detention', where a doctor saw her, but did not treat her. Eventually she was released. She had no menstruation for four months.

'Can what happened to Ayse Eker be justified?' asked AI's Report on Torture of 1973. 'There are those who must think it can. The country-by-country survey in this report indicates that many states in the world today deliberately use torture. Policemen, soldiers, doctors, scientists, judges, civil servants, politicians are involved in torture, whether in direct beating, examining victims, inventing new devices and techniques, senten-cing prisoners on extorted false confessions, officially denying the existence of torture, or using torture as a means of main-taining their power. And torture is not simply an indigenous activity, it is international; foreign experts are sent from one country to another, schools of torture explain and demonstrate methods, and modern equipment used in torture is exported from one country to another.

'It is commonplace to view our age as one of "ultra-violence". Much of the mass of information we are exposed to in the West reports catastrophes, atrocities, and horrors of every description. Torture is one of these horrors, but even in an age of violence, torture stands out as a special horror for most people . . . Within every human being is the knowledge and fear of·pain, the fear of helplessness before unrestrained cruelty . . . It is significant that torture is the one form of violence today that a state will always deny and never justify. The state may justify mass murder and glorify those that kill as killers, but it never justifies torture nor glorifies those that torture as torturers. And yet the use of torture has by all indications increased over the last few years . . .

'No act is more in contradiction of our humanity than the deliberate infliction of pain by one human being on another, the deliberate attempt over a period of time to kill a man without his dying.'

Why Torture?

AI's report, a special issue of the American journal *TIME* on torture as a state policy, a book, compiled in 1970 for the West German section of AI — to mention only a few publications — all try to analyze torture within the context of history and to discover the mental mechanism that makes men torturers. For here lies the key to success in a world-wide campaign for the elimination of torture, a battle which mankind must win if it wants to regain its humanity.

There is no doubt that man's maltreatment of a fellow being, human or animal, is a by-product of civilization. Like other beasts of prey, primitive man followed his instincts by attacking and swiftly killing an animal for food or another man as a dangerous enemy. Even human sacrifices were made, so to speak, 'humanely', without the victim's prolonged suffering. At any rate, no evidence of torture has been found in excavating pre-historic skeletons. Round holes in some skulls have turned out to be evidence of trepanning operations, carried out either for surgical purposes or to relieve patients from imaginary evil spirits in their heads. Thus man appears to have existed for several hundred thousand years without committing torture, practising it only during the last few thousand years; evidence from antiquity shows that it was done by highly cultured peoples and 'barbarians' alike.

There are roughly three headings under which the practice can be classified: as acts of vengeance on defeated enemies, as a prelude or accompaniment to executions, and as a means of extracting confessions or information. Any of these headings may, and frequently do, include intimidation, that of warning potential opponents or sinners by demonstrating to them what will happen to them if they antagonize the powers that be. The ancient Roman custom of prolonging the agony of prisoners condemned to death by crucifying them obviously served that purpose, while having them mauled to death by wild animals in the circus was also meant for the entertainment of a sadistic crowd.

And this element is perhaps the most worrying and complicated of the various features that pervade the whole subject of torture. The term sadism, meaning the sexual enjoyment of cruelty, is less than two centuries old; the Marquis de Sade from whose name it derives was a French army officer who was condemned to death for an 'unnatural crime', but escaped and ended his life in 1814 in a lunatic asylum. There he wrote novels and plays about his perversion — which, he assumed quite rightly, was shared by a good many other people — and tried to put it on some kind of philosophical basis. (The term for the complementary perversion, masochism, is even more recent; it is derived from the name of an Austrian novelist, Leopold von Sacher-Masoch, who about a hundred years ago described the sexual abnormality of finding pleasure in being tortured.)

From the examples of torture cases we have quoted it is evident that many torturers, if not most of them, get some perverted sexual pleasure out of their practices and frequently indulge in causing pain to the victims' sexual organs — preceded, as a rule by stripping them: their enforced nudity itself points to the torturers' sexual leanings. It may seem that the torturers are often selected by the authorities for the job because of these tendencies which make them particularly efficient. But this conclusion could be misleading; it is much more likely that the activity of torture brings out the dormant sadistic tendencies in primitive people while the more civilized ones have managed to sublimate or eradicate them during the process of growing up. Children, as we know, often tend to be cruel; some pull out a captured fly's wings or legs just to see how the insect manages without them. But it is only in puberty that the sexual element may come into cruelty if the boy's or girl's innate character has such inclinations. Another factor in infantile development is the anal phase, when the child derives pleasure from its excreta; some torturers'

63

preoccupation with their victims' anal zones points to what Freud called a 'fixation', an arrested mental development.

As to those who order torture as a means of policy to suit their ends, there does not seem to have been much emotional involvement throughout history. They are content to know that the torturers they employ do their work satisfactorily. There has never been any shortage of torturers, and their efficiency is usually heightened by the official assurance that they are acting in the interest of the nation or some religious belief. 'Dictatorial regimes,' said *TIME*, 'always manage to find enough people who — convinced of the righteousness of their cause — will maim or murder under orders from absolute authority.' There are, however, also certain types of torturers who enjoy 'getting their own back' after having suffered their own parents' brutality as children, or society's callous treatment as underdogs. Revenge may be their spur; revenge on those who were luckier, better educated, richer, more satisfied with their professional and home lives. Now the lucky dogs are in the power of the underdogs, helpless, squirming, crying for mercy — these arrogant intellectuals, successful businessmen, doctors and lawyers, and it's in a good cause they are made to suffer. What satisfaction for the torturers!

'The historical record implies that the capacity to torture is a potential common to man, or at least to some men in every human group,' says the AI survey. It points out that throughout the centuries, in western society, cycles of legalising torture and of abolishing it have followed each other, and that in some periods the attitudes of the nations towards torture have been ambiguous: 'Ancient Greece and Rome, from which the West traces much of its liberal and humanist tradition, forbade torture of the citizen. However, in Athens a slave's testimony was not considered reliable unless he had been tortured. In Republican Rome the same double standard applied, but under the increasingly despotic regimes of the Empire, the free man was subject to torture for an ever-widening range of offences.'

As the Romans had tortured the Christians to make them renounce their faith, the Christian Church, when it became the dominant spiritual power in Europe, condemned torture, and for a thousand years it was practically unknown in the western world. It was Pope Innocent IV in the thirteenth century who authorised it for use by the Inquisition, the Roman Catholic Church's 'Holy Office' — a court for dealing with the increasing unrest among the people. 'Heretics' were charged and made to confess. The assumption was that if a man was innocent, God would give him the strength to maintain his plea of innocence under torture while the guilty man would break down as he lacked divine assistance. The 'question', as interrogation under torture was called, was divided into several degrees, carried out in a special chamber and supervised by an official. 'Magistrates sat comfortably amidst the various paraphernalia,' says the AI report, 'duly noting the time, the weights and the measures of various tortures, and then recording the confessions which, not surprisingly, were generally forthcoming . . . Those justifying the use of torture by the Church argued that the mob was burning and torturing heretics, and the Church should bring it under control and thus minimise the use of torture.'

Contemporary pictures give an idea of torture practice. The victims were first flogged, then stretched on the rack and suspended by their wrists (*strappado*); thumbscrews, iron boots which crushed their feet, and burning coals over which they had to walk were further 'tests' to establish their guilt or innocence. As a rule, those found guilty were then handed over to the secular authorities for punishment according to the state laws — which frequently meant that they were burnt alive.

The notorious 'Spanish Inquisition' was set up with papal approval by Ferdinand and Isabella only a few years before what we call Modern Times began with Columbus' first journey of 1492. Headed by the Grand Inquisitor, Torquemada, it had the full backing of the state for the torture and burning of Marranos and Moriscos, converts from Judaism and Islam who were charged with secretly practising their former religion; later, the Spanish Inquisition turned against heretics suspected of Protestant sympathies.

Of course there were voices raised against torture; the strongest appeal for its abolition came from a German Jesuit, Friedrich von Spee, in the early seventeenth century who published a book after attending some major trials of women accused of being witches. Witch-hunts were frequent in Protestant England and America, which had been free of the Catholic Inquisition. In 1640, torture was abolished in England by law, though the torturing of suspected 'witches' continued for some time, while the soldiers roaming Central Europe during the Thirty Years' War amused themselves by torturing inhabitants of the countries they happened to be occupying. A favourite soldiers' game was to tie up peasants, smear the soles of their feet with salt, and let goats lick it off. The peasants were literally 'tickled to death'.

France made the use of torture a capital offence at the 1789 Revolution; most German states and even Russia abolished it early in the nineteenth century. The evil practice seemed to have gone for ever, at least in enlightened Europe, despite the many wars and revolutions which the Continent had to live through. The foundation of the Red Cross in 1864 — initiated by a Swiss banker, Henri Dunant, who had seen the sufferings of the wounded at the battle of Solferino — was a great victory for humanity. The Geneva Convention which was signed first by sixteen European countries and later by a further one hundred all over the world, compelled the signatory powers to exercise mercy in war and to treat prisoners humanely. It was even hailed as a first step to abolish war altogether.

The Victim Speaks

'The first blow makes the prisoner realize that he is helpless — and thus it contains the essence of all that will follow: they can hit me in the face with their fists, the victim feels with a kind of torpid astonishment; and he concludes with an equally torpid certainty: they will do to me what they like. Nobody knows about me outside, nobody will stand up for me . . . It does not mean much when someone who has never been beaten up makes the rhetorical statement that the first blow robs the prisoner of his human dignity. I am sure that it robs him of more: of something one might call his belief in the world. The expectation, the certainty to get help is one of man's fundamental experiences . . . Just a moment, says the mother to her child when it is in pain, there'll be a hot-water bottle, a cup of tea, you won't be allowed to suffer . . . Even on the battle-field the Red Cross helper finds his way to the injured. But with the first blow of the policeman's fist, from which there is no protection and which is not warded off by a helping hand, a part of our lives ends, never to be revived again.'

The writer was Jean Amery who was in the Belgian resistance during the second World War and fell into the hands of the German SS. The German book on torture we have mentioned quotes Amery and adds, 'These words show what it means when Amnesty can give at least to some prisoners the assurance: people know about me in the outside world, they stand up for me, they want to help me.'

The return of torture in our century, on a scale never reached even in the darkest Middle Ages, is one of the most tragic phenomena in human history, especially difficult to explain as it began in civilized, progressive Europe. There were many sporadic and individual cruelties in the civil war that followed the Russian revolution, but it was Mussolini's Fascism which, in the wake of his coup in 1922, first made torture again a state policy in aid of suppressing opposition. Already the term 'Fascism' — from the old Roman *fasces,* bundles of rods surrounding an axe as the emblem of authority over life and limb — represented a totalitarian threat to dissidents. The Duce's blackshirts invented a particularly sadistic technique: that of pumping the victim full of castor oil to purge him of his will to resist.

After Italy, the land of the arts, it was Germany, the 'country of poets and thinkers' as it liked to call itself, which turned to torture as an essential part of state policy. The first concentration camps, installed at once after Hitler's takeover in 1933, already had their torture chambers for political prisoners; ten years later, there were gas ovens for the mass murder of Jews and other 'inferior races'. Right from the start, political prisoners were treated with the utmost brutality. One case, that of Carl von Ossietzky, the editor of the leading German left-wing and pacifist weekly, *Die Weltbühne,* and a descendant of an old aristocratic Prussian family, may stand for the fates of untold thousands of tortured prisoners. The Nazi regime regarded him as a traitor because his journal had revealed Germany's illegal rearmaments to the world. A Red Cross delegation, led by the Swiss historian and diplomat Carl Jacob Burckhardt, saw Ossietzky at the Esterwegen concentration camp in 1935. Burckhardt wrote: 'Two SS men brought, or rather dragged and carried along a small man, a trembling, deadly pale creature which did no longer seem to feel anything. One eye was closed, the teeth had apparently been knocked out, and he was limping on one leg which had been broken and was badly healed. I asked him whether he had any messages for his friends. "Thanks," whispered Ossietzky, "tell them I am at the end. It will soon be over. It's all right that way." And he added, "I only wanted peace."'

The outside world tried to rescue him. He was awarded the Nobel Peace Prize, and the Nazis, faced with world-wide pressure of public opinion, had to release him into a hospital. The *Gestapo,* however, did not dare to let this half-dead torture victim go to Oslo to receive the prize, where he would have been seen as irrefutable evidence of Nazi barbarity. He died soon after his release, only forty-eight years old.

Spain was the third Fascist country to use torture more or less officially. Franco's *Falange,* the only political movement tolerated during his regime, vied with the old-established paramilitary *Guardia Civil,* the State Police, in torturing and murdering opponents. One would have thought that Spain's totalitarian nightmare would vanish overnight with Franco's death in 1975, but torture went on for another year or more, especially against the Basque separatists. Amnesty published a circular on torture in Spain, covering the last ten years of Franco, but many cases continued to come in throughout 1976, 'corroborated by hundreds of testimonies and even by formal denunciations which might be consigned to oblivion in the legal bureaucracy . . . It is the *Guardia Civil* which has been responsible for directing the majority of these operations. They have used all means of unimaginable tortures and have even introduced new ones'.

The special AI circular on Spain listed as the most common methods: the *banera* or bath — the victim is undressed, wrapped in a blanket, tied and plunged into a tub of filthy water containing the urine and vomit of other victims; the *quirofano* or operating table — the victim is stretched and tied on a table for beatings with hammers and truncheons; pins are inserted under the nails and testicles are beaten. Hanging by the wrists and electric shocks were other favourite methods of torture.

In the meantime, however, it seems that Spain has rejoined the ranks of those civilized nations which have not only outlawed torture, but also instituted effective legal means to suppress it. Yet can we be sure that even countries whose public opinion would not tolerate such practices do not use them under the cloak of military expediency? The Rev. Paul Oestreicher, Chairman of AI's British Section, spoke at the assembly of the Church of Scotland in 1977 about Amnesty's concern 'at the existence of a unit in the British Army which specializes in torture techniques'. This unit, he explained, is defended by the government on the grounds that it is 'needed to train soldiers to resist torture'. But, he asked, may this not open the door to potential abuse?

A rather complicated case has been Iran since a coup restored Shah Mohammed-Reza Pahlavi to the throne in 1953. He has made the greatest efforts to drag his ancient country into the twentieth century, using its income from oil exports to buy expertise and hardware for military, economic and social development from the West, where criticisms of Iran because of its treatment of political opponents are, therefore, uttered only *sotto voce* lest they may harm the big business deals with the Shah's government. Among those who have spoken out against Iran's violations of human rights and torture was the International Commission of Jurists; its observer, the French lawyer Jean Michel Braunschweig, who investigated Iranian conditions in 1976, estimated that the SAVAK (secret police) had 20,000 members and 180,000 paid informers. 'The country's repertory of torture,' he reported, 'includes not only electric shock and beatings but also the insertion of bottles in the rectum, hanging weights from testicles, rape, and such apparatus as a helmet that, worn over the head of the victim, magnifies his own screams.'

TIME correspondent Christopher Ogden, who accompanied the then U.S. Secretary of State Kissinger on his visit to Iran, spoke to the Shah about the torture allegations. 'We don't need to torture people any more,' the Shah told him. 'We use the same methods some of the very highly developed nations of the world are using, psychological methods. When faced with a confession of their comrades, the prisoners tell us everything.' The Shah also claimed there were 'no more than 3000 to 3500 political prisoners' in the country, and then went on to modify this statement: 'But they are not really political prisoners. They are Marxists; either terrorists, killers, or just people who have no allegiance to this country.' SAVAK, said *TIME*, seemed to concentrate its attention on writers, artists, and intellectuals. But perhaps the most terrifying feature of torture in Iran, as in Chile, was its 'institutionalization', the fact that it had become 'the almost private domain of huge, semi-autonomous police agencies,' *TIME* added. 'Once embroiled in the torture monolith, the individual has no appeal nor resource to the kind of legal authority provided by functioning courts.'

Amnesty watched the Iranian situation 'with deep concern', it reported in 1976. There had been an identifiable increase in the repression of opposition and an extension of SAVAK's activities to other countries where Iranians were living, in an attempt at preventing criticism of the Shah's regime. AI quoted estimates of the number of political prisoners, ranging from 25,000 to 100,000 (total population: c. 24 million). Yet in 1969, Iran acted as the host to an international conference on human rights, though 'a concern for human rights appears not to be reflected at all in its domestic practice'.

The earliest detailed statement of torture in Iran reached Amnesty in 1963, but Iranian dissidents alleged that it had been an established practice ever since the Shah's return to power ten years earlier. However, signed statements by victims have been extremely difficult to obtain; most of AI's information is contained in reports from observers who have attended trials of political prisoners — nearly all of whom retracted their confessions in court on the grounds that they were extracted under torture and therefore not valid. But the dead cannot make statements: the number of executions of political prisoners in Iran has been very high in recent years. For instance, during the first two months of 1976, fifteen executions were reported. But in the following year, 500 political prisoners were freed, probably due to international pressure.

Iran's neighbour, Iraq, has also been the cause of great concern for AI as 'one of the most serious violators of human rights in the Middle East'. Reports of arbitrary arrests, routine torture, and summary executions keep coming in, despite the official secrecy which surrounds them. The continuous power struggle in Iraq since the early 1960s, reported Amnesty, 'has been accompanied by purges, repression and physical elimination of all opposition' to the rulers that happened to be in charge. Torture allegations include bodily disfigurement and injuries inflicted by knives and other sharp instruments, often resulting in death. AI received the names of a number of such cases. A former Prime Minister, Abdul Rahmen al-Bazzaz, was said to have his arms and legs broken and to have lost an eye while imprisoned before his secret trial in 1968.

Iraq's Jews were singled out for particularly brutal repression. There had been 130,000 of them in the 1950s; now there are only a few hundred left. After the Arab-Israeli war of 1967, says the AI *Report on Torture*, 'small groups of Jews were arrested and tortured for a few days while questioned about their connections with Israel and Zionism, and released after payment of a fine by their community'. In 1971, a Western observer reported that an eleven-year-old girl had confessed to membership of a 'Zionist imperialist spy ring' after three days of rape and torture.

But Israel, too, has been charged with torture of Arabs, especially prisoners of war after the 1968 and 1973 wars. AI representatives visited the country and collected some evidence. Syria was also charged with torturing Israeli prisoners of war. 'Properly speaking,' said the Amnesty report, 'the treatment of wartime prisoners falls under the authority of the Red Cross rather than within the mandate of AI. Nevertheless, torture under any circumstances is the concern of AI.'

A Superhuman Task?

Considering that the sixty countries guilty of practising torture, according to the evidence collected by AI, make up nearly half the number of all U.N. member states, the task which Amnesty's CAT, the Campaign for the Abolition of Torture, has set itself seems almost superhuman. To be sure, much progress has been made since its beginnings on Human Rights Day, 1972. On the same day in 1975, the U.N. General Assembly adopted unanimously a 'Declaration on the Protection of All Persons from being subjected to Torture and Other Cruel, Inhuman or Degrading Treatment or Punishment', largely prompted by AI's evidence and efforts. Like the almost identical Article 5 of the original Human Rights Declaration adopted by the General Assembly of 1948, it was signed by all U.N member states — with only meagre practical results, as we have seen. 'The fact remains,' said AI's Annual Report for 1975-76, 'that too many governments subscribe to U.N. declarations and resolutions on human rights only on paper,' and the *Report on Torture*, covering the international scene at the same period, states candidly:

'At present there exist few effective ways of stopping torture. We have seen that only in the case of Greece was proof of torture authoritatively established by an intergovernmental judicial enquiry . . . South Africa and Brazil have received much international attention, but their governments have instituted no special internal enquiry to examine the use of torture, and sharply opposed any suggestion of an enquiry from the outside. Amnesty International has also investigated complaints from Aden and Israel. In none of these cases, apart from Greece, did the international enquiries receive cooperation from the local authorities. . .

'We have also noted, in the Report, certain new developments. In the first place, sophisticated methods of torture are being introduced in many countries. Interrogation techniques are being constantly refined. But torture is not being used for the extraction of information alone. It is also used for the control of political dissent. Often, the two main impulses are combined in one appalling practice. . . .It has also been applied in countries which are not at war and which, in some cases, have no broadly based domestic insurgencies to cope with. For instance, in Uruguay, Brazil, Indonesia, Greece and Turkey, the military are torturing civilians for reasons of domestic politics. This development reflects the growing involvement of the military in politics, and the increasing number of military regimes . . .

'Torture can occur in any society . . . It is misleading to suggest that poverty causes and wealth prevents torture. Torture exists in situations of sharp conflict.'

In its 1977 annual report, AI stated that according to recent information, continued clandestine torture was being used against political prisoners in eight black African countries: Morocco, Tunisia, Guinea, Uganda, Tanzania, Ghana, Ethiopia, and the Sudan. However, white-minority ruled South Africa and Rhodesia had now adopted torture of political detainees as 'official policy'. Altogether, the number of states guilty of violating human rights had in 1977 grown to two thirds of all U.N. members, the report added grimly.

One way of making the torturer's job more difficult would be strict codes of ethics for the legal and medical professions, prohibiting lawyers, judges, doctors and nurses from participating in torture practices — as suggested in an AI publication of draft codes by two eminent Dutch professional men, a lawyer and a physician (*Professional Codes of Ethics*, London, 1976). It also suggests a code for policemen against participation in torture. Beginnings to introduce such codes on an international level have been made by professional people who abhor torture. The trouble is that there will always be those who, from fear of losing their livelihoods or becoming torture victims themselves, will knuckle under to their dictatorial regimes, helping them with their dirty work. As to soldiers and officers, they will usually take refuge in the time-honoured excuse that they were 'only obeying commands'.

Psychological attacks on the practice of torture are an even less promising strategy, as the potential to torture is inherent in a great number of humans, and religious restraints have little effect in the face of official pressure. What a dictatorial state can do to overcome any ideological scruples has been shown most clearly by the Nazi regime; racial minorities, 'class enemies', and 'enemies of the people' are singled out by means of hate campaigns.

More effective may be the fear of retribution against the torturers. Even those who expect the downfall of their regimes, sooner or later, often rely on the difficulty of proving that a person has really been tortured, and some of the new, sophisticated techniques used by torturers in many countries have been introduced especially because they leave few, if any, visible traces. In 1974, AI's Danish Medical Group began using modern scientific methods to counter those of the torturers in a three-year research into the symptoms and effects of torture in order to make possible a better documentation of allegations. The Danish doctors and scientists not only examined dozens of ex-prisoners from Chile, Greece, and Argentina, but members of the team submitted them-

selves to new kinds of torture such as the 'shock baton', an elect-
rical instrument which had been used in Cyprus in the early 1970s.
It is a battery-operated police truncheon made commercially
in the U.S.A.

A most important general conclusion about the effects of
torture was that the worst of them were psychological and neuro-
logical; said the team's report (*Evidence of Torture: Studies by
the AI Danish Medical Group*, London, 1977): symptoms of
anxiety, irritability and often depression were common; mental
disturbance was evident in 60% of the examined Greeks and
Chileans. Loss of memory, impaired powers of concentration,
sleep disturbance and headaches were frequent. Some Greeks
who had suffered *falanga* showed paralytic and neuropathic
symptoms. One unexpected finding was the high percentage of
hearing disabilities, not necessarily as a result of beatings on the
ears, but possibly as 'part of a pattern of general torture symptoms'.
This field of research, AI added to the report, should be international, with shared resources and results, perhaps sponsored by
universities and medical foundations; and governments which
oppose torture should lend moral and financial support.

Another area of concern for AI has been 'the development and
use of intensive psychiatric and medical techniques designed to
control and, in some cases, permanently alter the behaviour'
of prisoners – popularly called 'brainwashing'. AI efforts at
identifying such techniques, frequently disguised by the authorities as psychiatric treatment for the prisoner's benefit, have not
yet been successful. However, AI has outlined what safeguards
for prisoners should be internationally adopted to abolish this
devilish abuse of psychiatry.

Altogether, it may appear that CAT can do little to stop torture
when it is commissioned by governments and carried out by bri-
gades of trained and specially equipped 'experts' – one of the
major symptoms of our age of collective and individual violence.
But so is the imprisonment of men and women for reasons of
political expediency – the original concern of Amnesty and the
cause of its existence. Yet the splendid support the movement
has been given internationally, the successes it has achieved, and
moreover the ideological and moral climate it has undoubtedly
created – is all this not reason enough to hope that its methods
might be equally successful in the fight against torture?

Basically, the weapons used in this fight are the same as those
forged in Amnesty's general campaign for the release of prisoners

of conscience. The cornerstones of the CAT programme are the 'urgent action campaigns' on behalf of named or potential victims of torture. AI has developed the capacity for rapid dispatch of telegrams and express letters, now carried out by an almost world-wide network of groups. 'Both the International Secretariat and AI national sections continuously streamline the procedures in order to deal with a growing number of urgent cases,' said the 1975-76 annual report. 'They try to minimize the loss of time and to mobilize, when necessary, the largest number of participants. At the same time, numerous organizations and individuals outside AI are regularly requested to intervene on behalf of detained persons and colleagues whom AI considers to be in danger of torture. Because of this improved organization, the urgent action system has become an instrument of selective response as well as a means of generating immediate mass appeals.'

These urgent action campaigns were at first concentrated on certain Latin-American countries where reports of torture were rife – Chile, Brazil, Uruguay and Argentina. The reasons for this were that anyone detained in these countries for political reasons was liable to be subjected to torture immediately after arrest, that political persecution had continued unabated or had intensified, as in Argentina after a military coup in 1976, and that AI continued to receive reliable information about arrests there quickly enough for immediate intervention. No fewer than one hundred and sixteen urgent action campaigns on behalf of some five hundred victims, or potential victims, were started in 1975-76 covering, apart from these Latin-American countries, also Tunisia, Iraq, Iran, Spain, South Africa, the Soviet Union, India, Pakistan, the Dominican Republic, Haiti, Taiwan, Bolivia, Paraguay, Nicaragua, Colombia and El Salvador. Those tortured, or in danger of torture, came from a wide range of social and occupational backgrounds. Some were persecuted because of their ethnic origin or political status, some were refugees from other countries, some had been taken hostage because of their relatives.

The results? Again, as with AI's general campaigns for the release of prisoners, success or failure is difficult to assess, but in some cases there were evident positive results such as releases or improved conditions. On the whole, the growing demand on AI to start urgent actions could be seen as a sign of their effectiveness, or at least of the faith which the friends and relatives of prisoners put in AI's campaigns. One refugee from Chile put it into these words: 'Amnesty's quick and effective mobilization to exert pressure and constantly to keep guard, to prevent the assassination of detainees under torture, has helped to save the lives of many Chileans.'

CAT also makes direct enquiries with the governments in countries which have been reported to use torture — several dozens of them in 1975-76. Missions were sent to a number of countries, seeking their governments' views regarding the implementation of the international agreements they had signed. But perhaps the greatest pressure of international public opinion can be exerted by an intense publicity campaign, such as that organized early in 1976 against torture practices in Uruguay. 'It demonstrates the potential of the AI movement as a whole for concerted international pressure on a government that systematically violated the fundamental human rights of its citizens,' said the annual report. 'The relative success of the Uruguay campaign in mobilizing and concentrating international public opinion on an unprecedented scale calls for an increase in AI's campaigning capacity on the international level.'

The paramount aim of CAT, however, is the awakening of the world's awareness and of people's resistance to the practice of torture. There is no doubt that the normal reactions of human beings, when faced with the facts and details of that practice, are revulsion and a desire to help abolish it. Christians, said Pope Paul VI at his 1978 New Year's reception for the diplomatic corps, 'must not remain silent and inactive when political prisoners are being tortured, when their bodies are subjected to irreparable damage and their souls to humiliating wounds'.

The effects of the first years of AI's campaign are encouraging, and they show that the methods have been well chosen. Torture is directly linked to politics because the governments concerned may regard it as necessary for their survival, so only the strongest pressure of world opinion can make them stop it. The torturers must understand that they may be held individually responsible for what they are doing — that there is no escape for them, no chance of hiding behind the 'I-only-did-my-duty' excuse. Individual responsibility was laid down nearly four decades ago, at the Nuremberg trials. 'Now,' said AI, 'the international community has to try to work out effective remedies for the prevention of torture.'

3

Watchdog
on the World

Worldwide Help
'Thanks to your intervention, I arrived in Paris on the 1st of May,
1969, after nearly three months' internment .... We owe our
freedom and liberty to the efforts of your organization, and it is
quite impossible to find the words for expressing our grateful-
ness . . . .'

As the 1960s, and with them the first decade of Amnesty's
work, were drawing to their end, letters such as this arrived daily
at the AI headquarters in London, at the national sections and at
individual adoption groups. The movement's help had become
truly world-wide. A man called Low Thai Thong, for instance, left
his Singapore prison after thirteen years of detention. The Swedish
group which had adopted him raised the funds for his fare to
London, where they flew to meet him and invited him to Sweden
to speak to those who had worked for his release. 'One of the most
striking features,' said the AI report for 1968, 'is the amount that
can be achieved by a group which extends its activities outside its
normal work. A recent example is the trip to Greece undertaken
by the member of a German group who, in a private capacity,
followed the route taken at George Papandreou's funeral, talking
to eye-witnesses. He was able to come in contact with the lawyers
of those sentenced to terms of imprisonment for shouting anti-
government slogans. The group had adopted one of these prisoners,
and as a result of this mission obtained much valuable information
on the trial proceedings and on the conditions of imprisonment
under which these people are now held. Other groups and sections
have raised money to send observers to trials, have provided legal
aid and have helped to finance missions undertaken by the Inter-

national Secretariat to investigate prison conditions . . . .'

A Rhodesian 'restrictee' wrote to an Australian group: 'When I received your letter I did not know what to do until, after thirty minutes, I read it again. This letter to me was something that I could call a dream because I could not believe it was mine . . . . After having satisfied myself that the letter was mine and read all that was written in it I went to my cell to pray and asked God to give you a long life in this world because I had given up that my family would ever have any people who could help them.'

Not all groups, AI admitted, were successful, and the frustration of writing letters for years with no replies received was daunting even for the most enthusiastic and conscientious of the members. Sometimes, AI's efforts even resulted in tragic failures, such as the arrest in Iran of one Hossein Rezai. He was merely seen accompanying a lawyer sent by the Austrian Section to investigate torture allegations. The lawyer was expelled from the country, but Rezai was sentenced to ten years' imprisonment at a secret trial by a military court.

Yet the overall picture of successes was highly encouraging. During the year 1969-70, two thousand prisoners were under adoption by eight hundred and fifty groups in twenty-seven countries, with an estimated £10,000 relief money distributed by them; and 520 prisoners had been released. AI's budget had risen to nearly £29,000. The annual Prisoner of Conscience Week, the first of which had been organized in November, 1968, as AI's contribution to the International Human Rights Year declared by the United Nations, was also most successful, and the postcards campaign was able to list a great number of releases of prisoners concerned — in Spain and India, in East Germany and Syria, in Kenya and Bolivia, in Poland and France and two dozen other countries, many men and women had been freed since 1965, when the postcards campaigns had begun.

Some of Amnesty's activities in those years may have been regarded as propaganda stunts, not quite in keeping with the seriousness and dignity of the movement. In Ireland and a few other countries, volunteers — teenagers or students — were locked in cages and publicly displayed to draw attention to the sufferings of prisoners of conscience. Forty-three national sections got ten thousand of their members to eat 'prisoners' meals' from prison bowls; they had the choice of either a Rhodesian dinner or a Russian one. The money saved by that detention diet was collected for AI funds. A branch in Kent even made a special Thespian effort in aid of

Amnesty, during Prisoner of Conscience Week, by putting on a play about the famous trial of William Penn, the Quaker and founder of Pennsylvania, which had taken place in London three centuries earlier.

Another special feature of Human Rights Year was that the International Amnesty Assembly in Stockholm, averse to concentrating the limelight on one Prisoner of the Year, chose three of them — the Greek woman Eleni Voulgari, sentenced to ten years' imprisonment in 1966, the African nationalist Daniel Madzimbamuto, interned since 1964 in Rhodesia, and the twenty-eight year-old Polish Jewess Nina Karsow, detained since 1966 and sentenced in October, 1968, to three years in prison by a Warsaw court for 'preparing to disseminate' her husband's political diary.

Two months later Nina Karsow was free and came to London with her husband, Szymon Szechter, also a Jew, and the blind writer of that diary of a dissident. He had lost his sight in battle when serving in the Red Army in the Second World War. Whether Nina's nomination as a Prisoner of the Year had made the Polish authorities release her and allow the couple to emigrate was not sure, but it was at least probable. They told AI on their London visit that they were 'full of praise for the Polish people' because, in the face of the official propaganda against Israel after the Six-day War, 'no-one is taken in by this — it fails to evoke any response'. The practical effect of the new propaganda line, said the couple, was that many Jews were 'removed from Polish public life and their jobs given to followers of the anti-semitic Minister of Security, General Moczar'.

A few years later, after a wave of strikes and riots had toppled Gomulka and brought Eduard Gierek to the leading position in party and government, AI was able to report that under him Poland had the smallest number of political prisoners in Eastern Europe; in 1969, the majority of prisoners of conscience, Jews as well as non-Jews, had been released. In fact, there have never been more than one to three Polish prisoners under Amnesty adoption since that fundamental change in the country's establishment. But neither did AI have any groups of members there, to say nothing of a national section. Wisely, AI has refrained from directing any propaganda to Poland, well aware of the strange dichotomy in its political climate. The Roman Catholic Church is as strong, and in the countryside even stronger, than the Communist Party. The people are, as Nina Karsow confirmed, unimpressed by official versions of world affairs, knowing that the government is forced to publish them to avoid a clash with its powerful neighbour, the Soviet Union. The country is simply a victim of geography. One has only to look at the map of Europe to understand why the Poles cannot arrange their way of life as they would want to. In the East lies Russia, in the West the hard-line German Democratic Republic, in the South Czechoslovakia, equally hard-line since the Soviet invasion of 1968 which crushed Dubcek's attempt at creating at least one country based on 'Socialism with a human face'. The Poles have to avoid a similar fate at all costs, and their policy in the 1970s has been to keep up Communist appearances while granting the people as much freedom as possible in political, personal, cultural and religious matters without provoking Moscow. They seem to be very good at maintaining their delicate balancing act.

In 1977, a 'Movement for the Defence of Human and Civil Rights (ROPCO)' was formed among students and intellectuals. Within a few weeks, information and consultation offices were opened in eight towns; they provide legal aid to people who complain about violations of human rights, and publish a monthly bulletin with a circulation of 5,000 copies. There seems to be no interference by the Polish authorities. Since the end of 1977, however, members of other groups such as the Social Self-Defence Committee (KOR, formerly the Workers Defence Committee) and the Society of Scientific Courses (TKN) have been increasingly subject to persecution and prosecution. The Polish authorities have used violence to break up private meetings in many towns in Poland, and individuals participating in lectures initiated by members of TKN and KOR have been charged with 'hooliganism' or with taking part in 'illegal meetings'.

The Dissidents

It is, of course, the Soviet Union on which AI's East European attentions have to be focussed; any changes in her treatment of opponents, or dissidents as one has come to call them, are usually echoed by similar changes in some other Warsaw Pact countries. Although Amnesty has never had reason to campaign against systematic physical torture in Russia, and although the wholesale murder of real or potential opponents under Stalin was a horror of the past, conditions in the 're-educational' labour camps and other penal institutions have been basically the same as described by Solzhenitsyn and other Russian writers. 'Soviet legality' was superficially observed at dissidents' trials; but Amnesty's requests for permitting their lawyers to attend them were consistently refused. Nor has there ever been, in AI's experience, an acquittal of a political defendant, and no Soviet court trying a person for his activities critical of the regime has ever rejected that charge.

The kind of problem AI is up against when dealing with the Soviet Union became blindingly clear in 1975. AI had prepared a one hundred and fifty page book with evidence on the treatment and conditions of prisoners of conscience in Russia, and submitted the text well in advance of publication to the Association of Soviet Jurists in Moscow for their comments. The reply which Martin Ennals, the Secretary General, received from them four months later was a masterpiece of brevity in the face of unpalatable truths: 'We would like to acknowledge that we are not eager to discuss what you call a book and that it is a vulgar falsification and defamation of Soviet reality and Socialist legitimacy.'

Civil liberties had never been a characteristic feature of Russian life. The first nineteenth-century dissident movement was that of the 'Decembrists', a group of mainly aristocratic officers who wanted to replace the autocratic tsarist regime by a liberal, constitutional monarchy; five of them were hanged when the revolt failed, and the rest banished to Siberia, the traditional place of exile for dissidents. The poet Pushkin, one of the sympathizers, was merely banished from Moscow and St. Petersburg. A quarter of a century later, in 1849, Russia's great novelist, Dostoyevsky, was arrested for being a member of a secret Socialist society, sentenced to be shot, but reprieved at the last moment and sent to a penal colony in Siberia for ten years.

Later, political offenders were incarcerated in the notorious Shlisselburg and Peter-Paul fortresses, but only some were sent to the criminals' forced-labour camps to work under conditions which few survived. Still, the total of political prisoners under the tsars was never more than a few thousand. But under Stalin, political oppression in Russia grew to such an extent that the often quoted figure of 'not less than ten to fifteen million who perished in the camps' has been generally accepted by historians.

When Amnesty began in 1961, the worst period was over. 'Our country has started along the path of cleansing itself from the filth of Stalinism,' wrote the Academician and eminent physicist, Andrei Sakharov, who was to receive the Nobel Peace Prize for his courageous human rights campaigns a few years later. 'In Chekhov's phrase, "drop by drop we are squeezing the slave out of ourselves", learning to express our views, not glancing over our shoulders at the boss and not fearing for our own lives.' But he admitted that the cleansing process was 'severely impeded' by neo-Stalinists in the key positions of power. The Soviet authoress Lydia Chukovskaya wrote in an open letter about the 'certificates of innocence' granted to those of Stalin's prisoners who had been lucky enough to survive. 'Excellent,' she said. 'They have returned. But where are those who were the cause of it all? Those who faked the charges against millions of people? . . . What are they doing today? . . . They are now in comfortable jobs or on big pensions.'

Thus the 'cleansing process' seemed to have stopped halfway through, while the persecution of dissidents continued, though on a very much smaller scale than under Stalin and on modified lines. Without doubt, the outside world's reaction to Russia's treatment of the opponents and critics of her regime has had a good deal of influence on the leading men in the Kremlin, and Amnesty's work in making the public aware of the situation has been increasingly effective.

One of the first major cases taken up by AI in 1966 was the prosecution of the writers Yuli Daniel and Andrei Sinyavsky. Unfortunately for Amnesty, their trial was widely exploited by political parties for propaganda purposes, which made AI's attempts at helping them more difficult. However, both were adopted as prisoners of conscience. The two dissidents had been accused of writing and circulating books containing 'anti-Soviet propaganda'. They were found guilty and sentenced to seven and five years respectively in hard-labour camps. Amnesty had launched a campaign against the trial taking place at all; it failed, and as usual no independent observers were admitted at the proceedings. The Swedish Amnesty section took action when Mikhail Sholokhov, the famous author of the *Silent Don* (now suspected of having cribbed the work from an unknown writer), was to receive the Nobel Prize for Literature in Stockholm. The Swedes handed to him a letter of protest against the 'new way of dealing with critics of the regime'.

In 1968, a Norwegian lawyer went to Moscow for AI to look at 'Soviet legality' in the cases of four young dissidents, Yuri Galanskov, Alexander Ginsburg, Alexei Dobrovolsky, and Vera Lashkova. According to Soviet law, pre-trial detention during a preliminary investigation may not, 'under any circumstances', last for more than nine months; yet Galanskov and Ginsburg had been held for a year. The Norwegian tried to enter the court room to observe the trial; the security guards turned him away. The sentences — 'pre-determined', as AI called them — put the prisoners in corrective labour camps; Galanskov, a poet, got seven years for his active defence of Sinyavsky and Daniel. He developed a duodenal ulcer, but the administration of the camp (in Mordovia) refused to allow him to receive the special food, such as honey, sent by relatives, and he was forced to continue working an eight-hour day. His mother's complaints to the camp commander were answered with the assertion that Galanskov was not ill but just 'a work-shy hooligan'. After four years at the camp, his ulcer burst, and there had to be an emergency operation. It was not carried out by the camp doctor, but by a fellow prisoner without any surgical experience. Galanskov died, at the age of thirty-three.

The dissidents have their own underground 'press' called *samizdat*, typewritten newsletters which they circulate amongst their friends; since 1968, there has been a *samizdat* 'journal' called *A Chronicle of Current Events*, devoted to recording violations of human rights in the Soviet Union. Copies were smuggled out of Russia to the West, and AI began to publish regular English-language editions in 1971. These reports have been the major source of information on the treatment of dissidents in the USSR, and they make very depressing reading. Many names from the *Chronicle* are among the several hundreds of Soviet prisoners of conscience adopted by Amnesty over the years. Whole groups of people have been persecuted — Ukrainians and Armenians who had protested against the 'Russification' of their countries, Jews accused of campaigning for 'Zionism and Imperialism', and two hundred Baptists arrested for merely asserting their constitutional rights to freedom of religion and for giving religious instruction to children. A list with their names reached Amnesty in 1967 — an 'almost unprecedented document', as the annual AI report called it: 'It is something of a mystery how those who collected the information, which covers an area stretching from Byelorussia to Central Asia, were able to do so successfully.' Most of the arrested Baptists were given labour-camp sentences from three to five years.

Then there are the Crimean Tartars, a large ethnic group expelled wholesale by Stalin during the second World War, when he charged them with having collaborated with the Germans who had been occupying the Crimea. Ever since, they have demanded to be allowed to return from exile in Asia. Typical of their treatment was a mass arrest in 1968 when the Tartars gathered in an Uzbek city to celebrate Lenin's birthday: soldiers and policemen surrounded the revellers, drenched them with some 'poisonous liquid' from a water cannon, beat them up and shoved them into prison vans.

Andrei Sakharov has been the most intrepid watchdog of the outrages of 'Soviet legality'. Constantly harassed by the authorities, he has contributed the bulk of the material to the *Chronicle of Current Events*. In 1970, he founded the — of course unofficial — 'Committee of Human Rights' in Moscow, together with two other physicists. They inundate the legal authorities with protests in all cases of violations of human rights of which they are informed, circulate evidential documents, try to send their members as observers to political trials — needless to say, rarely with any success: the guards outside the courts, the KGB men inside have often handled Sakharov and his friends very roughly.

Psychiatric 'Treatment'

'I complained of feeling poorly after a dose of haloperidol, and asked that the dose be reduced. This led to my being prescribed even more aminazine than I was already receiving . . . . During a hunger strike in January, 1971, (I had been given aminazine ever since my arrival) I felt steadily worse and worse, and after making a complaint, I began to get aminazine injections in the maximum dose . . . . I couldn't sleep at all; yet the same dose was administered to me for twelve days in a row, until they became convinced that I was still not sleeping, and that the injections had not made me give up my hunger strike . . . . I have been given two tablets of haloperidol twice daily . . . . This medicine makes me feel more awful than anything I have experienced before; you no sooner lie down than you want to get up, you no sooner take a step than you're longing to sit down, and if you sit down, you want to walk again — and there's nowhere to walk.'

The writer of this letter, which reached AI through undisclosed channels, was Vladimir Gershuni who, still a teenager, had been sentenced to ten years in a labour camp as a member of an anti-Stalin youth group in 1949. He served his full term, although Stalin died in 1953. After his release Gershuni, working as a bricklayer, became active in the human rights movement and was arrested again in 1969 when the police found *samizdat* documents on him, the most incriminating being leaflets in defence of Major-General Grigorenko, a well-known dissident who had recently been sent to a mental hospital. Gershuni, too, was duly diagnosed by forensic psychiatrists as being of unsound mind, and was not allowed to attend his trial. The court decided that he should be taken to a 'special' psychiatric hospital. This was the newly opened prison hospital at Oryol, south of Moscow. For all we know he may still be there.

His case was only one of a great number of similar ones which had been reported to AI and whose victims were adopted. Among the first had been Zhenya Belov, a student, whose story was brought to London in 1965 by four British friends of hers. They described her as an enthusiastic Communist who had written to the Party suggesting certain improvements in Soviet life. As a result, she was put in a mental hospital as a 'schizophrenic'.

As we know, locking up critics of the establishment in lunatic asylums had already been a traditional way of getting rid of them in tsarist Russia. Strangely enough, as one of the publications of the Moscow Human Rights Committee stated, 'during the widespread Stalinist repressions many persons were saved by psychiatric hospitals, and, whatever the present situation, one must not forget this'. At least until the mid-1930s, psychiatrists' findings had been used very liberally to free numerous people from criminal prosecution.

In 1961, however, the old custom was legalised for the first time by a new regulation under the heading, 'On the Immediate Hospitalization of Mentally Ill People representing a Social Danger', and the Soviet judges used to the official jargon understood well enough that 'social' meant 'political', and what was expected of them. So did the forensic psychiatrists. Officially, however, being locked up in a mental hospital does not rank as a punishment, for the Soviet criminal code states that mentally ill persons cannot be sentenced for crimes they may have committed. On the other hand, there are no official regulations on the kind of 'treatment' the supposedly insane critics of the regime should get, nor on the duration of their sojourn in the hospital.

Even before their trials, dissidents are frequently sent to mental hospitals; thus the four — perfectly sane — intellectuals Galanskov, Ginsburg, Dobrovolsky, and Lashkova spent some time at the Serbsky Institute for Forensic Psychiatry in Moscow, where they were given drugs which made them speak 'oddly' in court. Drugs have also been used to draw out confessions from prisoners before their trials.

In 1967, a letter by the wife of a thirty-year-old Moscow artist, Victor Kuznetsov, appeared in the Italian paper *Il Popolo*; it had originally been sent a year earlier to *Izvestia*, which of course never published it. She complained that her husband had been speaking at a discussion in Moscow University, with the result that he was dismissed from his post, picked up by a police van one morning at 8 o'clock, and delivered to a psychiatric hospital 'for consultation

and diagnosis'. His case sheet was subsequently sent to his wif

'Kuznetsov, Victor Vasilyevich. Expresses wild ideas on human relation Considers the attitude of his relatives incorrect . . . . Considers the attitud to him at work to be incorrect. Reacts wildly to the attempts of oth people to speak. Expresses critical views about the government. Criticiz various sorts of government measures . . . '

Obviously, he was mad, implied the case sheet. But he was dia nosed as fit for release by an expert psychiatric commission in th Kazan hospital where he had been sent. When this recommenda tion reached the local court, the procurator requested, 'in view o the gravity of Kuznetsov's guilt', that his confinement in the hos pital should be prolonged. This was done, but after his eventua release he was arrested again in 1969 when a draft for a new Soviet Constitution was found in his house.

An Amnesty member was received by the director of the Serbsky Institute (which is subordinate to the Ministry of Health) in 1966 several young intellectuals had been reported as spending a pre-tria period there. An armed guard was at the entrance of the Institute The director confirmed that the young writer Vladimir Bukovsk was currently being 'treated' before going on trial. He was, howeve released, only to be re-arrested some months later and sentenc to three years' imprisonment for organizing a students' demonst tion. There was no suggestion in court of any mental disturbar of Bukovsky.

Leonid Plyushch, a cybernetics expert and dissenter who later allowed to leave the Soviet Union, said that he had been k at the Dniepropetrovsk Special Hospital for two and a half y after a diagnosis of 'lingering schizophrenia with reformist d sions'. He was given various drugs, including heavy doses of sul which caused 'such intense discomfort that all you could do endlessly search for a new position', an experience similar to described by Gershuni.

In 1970, the eminent Soviet biologist Dr. Zhores (Ja Medvedev was arrested, declared insane, and sent to the K Psychiatric Hospital. The head doctor there, according to M dev, 'spent a long time trying to convince me that to eng "publicist" writing in addition to one's normal professional scientific or otherwise, was a sign of a split or "disassociated sonality. "In time, of course, the hospital will discharge yo doctor said, "but you must completely stop all this other a or you will inevitably end up back here." '

AI started at once a 'postcards campaign' for him, but his release after only three weeks' detention seems to have been the result of the angry protests of many Soviet scientists. His twin brother, Roy, a Marxist historian, quoted in a submission to the Moscow Human Rights Committee in 1971 some of the 'expert diagnoses' of psychiatric illness based on symptoms such as: 'an obsessive mania for truth-seeking', 'wears a beard', 'meticulousness of thought', 'considers the entry of Soviet troops into Czechoslovakia to have been aggression', and — surely the most bizarre symptom of madness in a Communist state — 'thinks he must devote his life to the ideals of Communism'.

Amnesty, which has adopted many hospitalized dissenters, is well aware of the fact that most of these prisoners held under the obviously spurious pretext of mental illness would otherwise suffer even much greater hardships in hard-labour camps. But the conclusion that they had been put in lunatic asylums for their own benefit would probably be wrong. The problem is rather complicated, and one has to attack it at its basis: the denial of the human right to speak one's mind without being persecuted in any way. A little light may be shed on the matter by a remark reported to have been made by a psychiatrist to Vladimir Borisov, a Leningrad electrician, twice confined to mental hospitals because of the opinions he had expressed: 'Listen, Borisov, you're a normal fellow and I'm sure you don't want to be sent to a madhouse. Why don't you change your views?'

To include the Soviet Union in the international family of countries with Amnesty branches had seemed an impossible dream; still, it was worth an attempt. In 1974, Secretary General Martin Ennals and two other leading men of the movement went to Moscow for talks with members of the Committee of Human Rights, which had expressed the wish to join AI and form an adoption group, promising to stick rigidly to the principles of the movement. This meant that they would, in their work for Amnesty, refrain from any involvement in Soviet politics. In September, 1974, the International Executive recognized the Moscow group as an AI branch; thus the first representation of Amnesty in Eastern Europe had been established.

Valentin Turchin, a physicist and computer specialist, was elected chairman, and Andrei Tverdokhlebov, a young physicist, became the secretary. Other founder members were the Ukrainian writer Mikola Rudenko, the biologist Kovalyov, the physicist Yuri Orlov, the mathematician Albrecht, and Sakharov's wife Helena.

The international secretariat gave them the usual three prisoners for adoption, one in Spain, one in Sri Lanka, and one in Yugoslavia. The relevant documents were dispatched from London; they never arrived, nor did any other communications after November, 1974. Turchin charged the authorities with having confiscated his mail. Worse, Kovalyov was arrested; Tverdokhlebov's flat was searched twice, and eventually he, too, was arrested by the KGB on his way to work. On the same day, Rudenko was detained in Kiev, but soon released under the condition that he would not leave town; he was also excluded from the Ukrainian Writers' Association because he had 'joined a bourgeois organization', and threatened with prosecution for having disseminated anti-Soviet material. The charge was eventually dismissed, but Kovalyov was brought before a court and sentenced to seven years' imprisonment. Orlov, too, was eventually arrested; he had also been the chairman of the 'Citizens' Group' monitoring Russia's performance under the Helsinki Agreement of 1975. He was still in gaol in 1978, awaiting trial. Tverdokhlebov was brought to trial and sentenced to five years' 'internal exile' for disseminating 'fabrications known to be false which defame the Soviet State and social system' — in other words: for his activities as the Moscow Amnesty group secretary.

That, to all intents and purposes, was the end of AI's Soviet branch. Turchin, who had lost his job at a Moscow computer institute after speaking up in defence of Sakharov who had again been publicly attacked, received an offer from Columbia University to teach mathematics there, but he did not want to leave the Soviet Union. In the autumn of 1977, however, he arrived in Vienna: 'I was compelled to leave,' he said. 'I had resisted pressure from the authorities for more than three years.'

He was only one of quite a number of dissidents subjected to the new anti-dissident policy of the Soviet leadership — that of letting them go or throwing them out. It had begun with Solzhenitsyn, Zhores Medvedev, and others in the mid-1970s, and has since continued steadily. 'The authorities want to destroy the dissident movement,' said Naum Meiman, a member of the human rights group, 'by sending some to the East, to Siberia, and some to the West.' The oddest barter deal in human lives was made early in 1977 between two totalitarian states — Communist Russia and Fascist Chile: Bukovsky was 'exchanged' for the former Communist leader, Luis Corvalan.

The very month, October 1977, when East and West met to review the working of the Helsinki Agreement, was selected as the time for a new crackdown on the whole human rights movement in the Soviet Union. Alexander Ginsburg was arrested again; so was Anatoli Shcharansky, who had acted as a link between the dissidents and the Jews who had so far been denied exit visas to Israel. Three of the ten members of the human rights group were exiled to the West, others to Siberia. On Soviet television, Yuri Andropov, the head of the KGB, told viewers what, in the opinion of the Politbureau, those dissidents were: 'The victims of political or ideological aberrations, religious fanaticism, nationalistic quirks, personal failure and resentment, and in many cases individual psychological instability . . . . Dissidents who maintain contacts with Western diplomats and correspondents will be treated as imperialist agents.'

Another view of the renewed action against the dissidents was expressed by a foreign diplomat in Moscow: 'Human rights are an infinitely more dangerous weapon against the Soviet regime than the entire arsenal of American strategic weapons. The men in the Kremlin can't be secure in their continuing control if human rights are respected.' But the most determined assault of the Kremlin on Shcharansky, Ginsburg, and other members of the Helsinki monitoring group was still to come — in the summer of 1978.

Prisoners for Cash

No doubt, the Soviets, worried about the marked increase of dissident activity also in other East European countries, wanted to set a firm example for their satellite nations. As usual, the German Democratic Republic was most eager to comply with Moscow's wishes. A number of East German dissidents were exiled to West Germany, and certainly the majority of them were not sorry to go. One of the exceptions was the most popular satirical song writer and performer, Wolf Biermann, who had been banned from singing and publishing his work for years. He was in 1976 permitted to go on a tour in the Federal Republic, but deprived of his GDR citizenship while he was away so that he could not return. Yet he would have liked to do so, if only to rub his masters' noses in their imbecilities and iniquities (his songs were privately circulated among the East Germans).

Expatriating dissidents, Russian style, was not East Germany's only way to get rid of them. Her favourite method had been for a long time to sell them for hard-currency cash. This has only been possible because, in contrast to the other Soviet-bloc countries, there is always an interested customer — West Germany. Needless to say, the GDR authorities have never told their people about these deals; the scheme seems to have operated since 1967 when Bonn paid about £3 million in deutschmarks for thirty-seven political prisoners, including fourteen women. The numbers of prisoners sold has fluctuated widely throughout the years. In 1972-73, there was in the GDR a general amnesty, followed by a steep rise in the annual figures of 'sales', reaching to less than 1300 prisoners in 1976. Then the number of GDR citizens transported to the West German border (and, of course, deprived of their citizenship) fell again; in 1977, it was estimated at 180, for whom an undisclosed sum was paid. Released dissidents not selected for sale do not have an easy life in the GDR; they and their families are subjected to all kinds of restrictions. Teachers, for instance, and other professional people are no longer permitted to work in their professions, but forced to do poorly paid manual jobs. They are frequently restricted in their places of residence; they receive no compensation for property confiscated at the time of arrest; their children are often barred from higher education. Many of those who were imprisoned for attempting to flee the country try it again, and are promptly sent back to gaol.*

Already in 1966, AI appointed a special team to investigate prison conditions in East Germany. It was headed by Karin O'Donovan, the honorary secretary of the Irish Amnesty section. Amnesty has, of course, never taken any part in the buying-out scheme operating between the two Germany's, as it has, on principle, 'never acquiesced in any barter of prisoners' fates'.

Czechoslovakia has always been Amnesty's concern since its campaign for the release of Archbishop Beran in the early 1960s, and especially since the abrupt ending of the 'Prague spring' under Dubcek in 1968 — the invasion of the Warsaw Pact troops was followed by the removal of all Dubcek sympathisers from public and Party positions and their systematic relegation to manual labour. A series of dissidents' trials began in 1971-1972; AI nominated a delegate to observe the proceedings, but he was refused an entry visa to the country.

However, according to AI's information, the number of prisoners of conscience thereafter decreased from between two and three hundred to about fifty to a hundred. But a new wave of arrests and personal prosecutions started in January, 1977, after the

---

* West Germany also bans its dissidents, the Communists, from 'public service' jobs — from administrative work down to that of a postman.

founding of a human rights movement among the intellectuals, artists, and professional citizens, who published (privately, of course), a manifesto under the title 'Charter 77'.

The Czechoslovak leadership seemed to have been thrown into a state of near-panic by this document which, after all, merely reminded them of their obligations under the various human rights agreements they had signed, and especially of the terms laid down in the Helsinki treaty of 1975. More than eight hundred people signed the Charter; a great number of them were simply removed from their jobs, banned from their professional associations, and reduced to whatever unskilled work they could get. A sad and apparently typical case was that of a Mr. Karel Kyncl, the former correspondent of Radio Prague in New York who had been called back and sentenced to twenty months' imprisonment in 1971. After his release, the only job he could find was that of an ice-cream seller at a Prague railway station. He lost that job, too, when he was found to have signed the Charter 77. Even his son, a photographer, was penalised by being banned from university study; he had to become a nightwatchman to help his family. Kyncl showed considerable courage in permitting an English television team to film an interview with him clandestinely on a deserted country road somewhere in Bohemia; the film was then shown on western television programmes in connection with the tenth anniversary of Russia's 1968 invasion of Czechoslovakia, which ended the 'Prague spring' under Dubcek.

Eventually, the Czechoslovak authorities decided to stage a show trial of four prominent dissidents, three of them Charter signatories — although that irritating document was not allowed to be mentioned in court. The accused were a former theatre director and Party member who had spent the war years as a refugee in London; a journalist who had already served three prison sentences within seven years for maintaining 'conspiratorial links' with foreign diplomats; another former theatre director, who had also been in prison before; and a well-known playwright who had acted as a spokesman for the Charter group. The sentences were comparatively mild: from suspended fourteen and seventeen month terms to 3½ years in prison — though the Czechoslovak leader, Gustav Husák, had declared only in 1975 that there would be no more political trials in his country. Some Charter supporters, among them the former Foreign Minister, Jiri Hajek, issued on the Charter's first anniversary in 1978, an appeal that all political detainees should be freed.

AI adoption groups have been active on two or three dozen cases of prisoners in Czechoslovakia, but observers have never been admitted to the trials.

The Country of 35,000 Prisoners

The classic remark of a British Prime Minister when Hitler threatened Czechoslovakia — 'A far-away country of which we know little' — has gone down into the annals of history as a notable example of a statesman's unconcern in the face of a problem which, he hoped, would go away by itself. Since then, the world has learnt the lesson that it may turn a blind eye to the problems of the time only at its peril.

Yet to many people in the West, Indonesia is still a very far-away country of whose mere existence we know little; still less about the inconceivable extent of the oppression which its people are suffering. It has now about one hundred and thirty five million inhabitants, with an adult population of around 40 million. The Dutch were the colonial masters of these islands between the South China Sea and the Indian Ocean — among them some with 'romantic' names such as Java, Sumatra, Borneo — for three centuries. In 1949, after the Second World War and the Japanese occupation, an independent Republic of Indonesia was established. The great majority of the people are Muslims; other religious groups are the Hindus, the Christians, and the Buddhists.

Political imprisonment in Indonesia began under Dutch colonial rule. The struggle for independence by Indonesian nationalists was met by severe repression, and, starting in the 1920s, the Dutch colonial government maintained a penal colony in the interior of West Irian, to which political prisoners were transported. In the years following Independence, however, there was virtually no political imprisonment in Indonesia. But erosion of parliamentary democracy began in 1957 when President Sukarno, a former engineer and anti-Dutch nationalist who had been imprisoned by the colonial forces, established martial law; later, in 1959, he introduced a type of authoritarian rule, described as 'guided democracy,' in which the elected parliament was replaced by an appointed legislature and the government's executive power was greatly increased.

Local rebellions in the late 1950s were followed by widespread arrests, but during the early 1960s most of the several thousand people detained were released under a general amnesty. The Sukarno government still kept a number of political opposition leaders and many others who had criticised government policies in prison.

With the promulgation of martial law the Army expanded its influence and became closely involved in political and economic affairs. During this period, the Indonesian Communist Party (PKI) was also growing in strength: in the 1955 elections, the PKI had polled 16.4% of the votes; by 1965 the party's membership exceeded three million, and well over ten million belonged to mass organisations under communist leadership. The PKI had the largest membership of any communist party outside of the Soviet bloc and the People's Republic of China.

For years President Sukarno used the Army and the PKI to counterbalance each other. When, in September 1965, a group of middle-ranking military officers attempted to destroy the leadership of the Indonesian Army, the Army leadership chose to interpret the 'coup' as the first step towards setting up a communist government, the officers who led it as chosen instruments of the PKI, and every communist and left-wing organisation as implicated in it. Led by General Suharto, the Army moved quickly to suppress the coup, carrying out a massive and violent purge in which it is estimated that around a million people identified or suspected of being affiliated with left-wing organisations were summarily killed and more than half a million were thrown in prison without trial. In 1966 President Sukarno, who had tried in earlier speeches to stem the tide of persecution and who had initiated investigation into massacres of prisoners, was forced to sign over his executive powers to General Suharto; his cabinet ministers were arrested and his administration was replaced with a military regime which moved to purge itself of all 'pro-Sukarno elements'.

In October 1965 General Suharto set up a 'Command for the Restoration of Security and Order' with himself as the Commander. The Command, known as *Kopkamtib*, was given wide powers to investigate and control political activity in the republic and had at its disposal all the resources of the Army. Their overriding task was the suppression of Communism in Indonesia. Suspected political deviants were arrested under a 1963 presidential decree which defined as subversive activities, among others, the 'dissemination or arousing of hostility' against the government, the 'demonstration of sympathy with an enemy of the Republic' and even the possession of maps or pictures of military buildings, to say nothing of acts of sabotage or espionage. Innumerable prison camps were set up, vast masses of detainees were sent there, most of them to be kept without trial. Arrests under this decree are still taking place, and despite partial amnesties and releases during the 1970's, there are at least 25,000 political prisoners in the Indonesian archipelago.

Right from its beginnings, AI took up cases of Indonesian political prisoners, and several reports on their fates and conditions were published over the years. The first AI mission to Indonesia in 1969, by the distinguished Australian lawyer Professor Julius Stone, was followed by a visit of Sean MacBride, which had been arranged by the German section during President Suharto's visit to Bonn in 1970. But after this mission, visas for Amnesty lawyers were refused. Then again, in 1975, an AI delegation headed by another eminent Australian barrister was allowed to get to Jakarta. However, all the ministers and officials they wanted to see, refused or found they had no time. In that year — International Women's Year — AI sections organized campaigns emphasizing that Indonesia stood out as the country with probably the largest number of female political prisoners. On Indonesian Independence Day in 1975, AI petitions for the release of untried political prisoners, signed by one hundred and thirty Swedish parliamentarians, thirty-one thousand West Germans and several thousand Austrians, were handed to the Indonesian embassies in Stockholm, Bonn and Vienna. A coordinated international campaign took up the cases of the tens of thousands of prisoners who had spent up to ten years without trial; in the U.S.A., Australia, the Netherlands, Canada and other countries, the AI sections and groups achieved extensive coverage by the press, radio, and television. Six months later, in the spring of 1976, AI launched yet another international campaign for the release of Indonesia's women prisoners; many national sections, among them the Swiss, Belgian, Japanese, and Nigerian, sent appeals and petitions to Jakarta. In the autumn of that year, AI publicized the truth about the Indonesian government's so-called transmigration programme, 'the forcible transportation of prisoners to permanent penal colonies (for instance, on the island of Buru) on the pretext that this amounts to the "release" of political prisoners'.

The following year, AI published some of the abundant material it had collected in a major report on the Indonesian situation. It contained a number of cases so tragic that the government of Jakarta now stood in the dock as one of the world's most brutal gang of political oppressors.

A Blind, Deaf and Dumb Prisoner
There is, for instance, the case of Bambang Supeno, adopted by Amnesty. He is blind, deaf and dumb, and was arrested after the

unsuccessful coup in 1965. Bambang Supeno was detained, without trial, in Surakarta Prison. Any inquiries about the charges against him were ignored by the authorities. 'He may have been detained because of some suspected offence never proven in court,' said the report, 'or else because of an administrative error, or as a result of completely arbitrary action on the part of some soldiers.' The unfortunate man was still in prison at the time when the report appeared, and there are many more prisoners, who, like him, are victims of circumstance.

The anti-Communist hysteria which was responsible for the waves of arrests in 1965 and 1966 has never been paralleled anywhere in the world. People were picked up *en masse* by local military commanders without any legal requirements such as warrants of arrest. The military could not cope with the vast numbers taken into custody, and recruited civilian helpers known for their anti-leftist views to assist with interrogations. This process was highly arbitrary; one word or even the pointing of a finger was sufficient to have a prisoner taken away to be killed. Interrogation was intended as revenge and a means of terrorizing people. Torture was common and cruel. Ten years later, the head of the state security agency, Admiral Sudomo, gave an interview on Dutch television in which he stated that 'more than half a million people' had been killed after the attempted coup. Other estimates by independent observers put that figure much higher — up to more than a million.

'Mere statistics alone do not adequately describe the terrible experience of many people in the aftermath of the 1965 events,' says AI. There was the case of a man, arrested in early 1966, and his child:

'Initially his wife was afraid to make enquiries about him for fear that she too were arrested. Later, she searched for him and failed to find him. The prisoner could not contact his family. The wife could not support her children and was forced to abandon their family home. She assumed her husband was dead.

'One of their children was six years old when his father was taken away. He was especially devoted to his father. He became emotionally disturbed and obsessive about finding his father, and walked the streets asking strangers whether they had seen him. In early 1974, eight years after his father's arrest, he had grown into a boy of 14 who was mentally retarded, still obsessive and wandering from home in search of his father, showing passing strangers an old photograph. One day he walked by Salemba Prison in Jakarta and showed the photograph to a passing prison official. The boy thus found his father, after eight years. He was a prisoner at Salemba . . . .'

An Indonesian writer, Usamah, wanted to do his bit against the Communists after the abortive coup of 1965, and volunteered to become a civilian member of a military interrogation team. On several occasions he had to interrogate his own friends; the first was a woman schoolteacher who, during interrogation, indicated that she knew him. This frightened Usamah, and he ordered the guards to 'torture the bitch'. The woman was tortured and signed a confession. Then came Usamah's family doctor, and Usamah tried to avoid a confrontation:

> 'I suggested to my superior that he should appoint someone more scientifically minded to work on the doctor. The commander misunderstood me and sent a torturer. I watched the familiar gangland scene without being able to do anything to stop it. He screamed for mercy as the blows of the belt buckle rained down on him.'

Later, Usamah had to interrogate a former classmate of his, a girl called Sri. He had to identify her, and she was taken away with thirteen other prisoners to be killed. Among them was also the schoolteacher he had ordered to be tortured. He had to go with the prisoners and the soldiers to a village where they were to be executed:

> 'The soldiers shouted abuse at the prisoners, and their shouts grew more hysterical and reverberated throughout the village as the fourteen prisoners walked slowly to the river's edge. Sri cried as soon as she was taken off the truck. The teacher was calm, although her face was as bitter as a dry lemon. They were lined up in rows at the steep bank of the river. I can still hear them weeping . . . .'

Pramoedya Ananta Toer, born in 1925, was also a writer before his arrest in 1965, but unlike Usamah he had never tried to assist the Suharto regime. He was a novelist, essayist and critic of considerable literary standing, and selections from his work are still prescribed reading in Indonesian schools. Alas, he has been unable to write anything since becoming a political prisoner, for all prisoners are denied pencil and paper.

He is now an AI adoptee among the fourteen thousand prisoners on the island of Buru, scheduled for permanent incarceration without charge or trial. It is his third spell of imprisonment. Each arrest was made under a different administration: first by the Dutch colonial government when he fought for Indonesian independence in the nationalist movement in 1945 (he began to write his first book in a Jakarta prison); then by the Sukarno authorities in 1960 after he had published a popular historical work on Indonesia, which displeased the government and was banned; and five years later by General Suharto's men because he was considered a Marxist. He was, however, never a member of the Communist Party. His arrest brought to an end his work on an encyclopaedia; the arresting soldiers threw his wife and eight children out of their house, and a mob was allowed to ransack and destroy his books, manuscripts, and all the material he had collected for his work. Pramoedya's wife, who is gravely ill with tuberculosis, lives with the children in poverty in Jakarta; they were never allowed back to their house. Three of his brothers are also political prisoners; the wives of two of them have divorced their husbands.

A group of journalists was permitted to visit Buru in 1971. They saw Pramoedya, and he told them about his predicament as a writer without pencil and paper. 'I want to return to my home in Java,' he told them. 'I was free in everything, thinking and talking and working . . . . I have lost my freedom, my family, my work. I want to write, and one day I will write again.'

Women and Children behind Barbed Wire

The official reason for detaining that immense number of people as political prisoners is that they are Communists. But among the detainees at Buru were a boy who was twelve when he was arrested and a girl who was thirteen, and probably many more who could scarcely have taken part in political activities because of their age. Sugiyah, adopted by AI and said to have been released, was among the youngsters who were recruited into the campaign of confrontation with Malaysia by a PKI youth organisation in 1965. They were trained near an Air Force base in Lubang Buaya — which shortly afterwards became the headquarters of the coup leaders. Here some generals, kidnapped by the rebels, were taken and killed. Anyone who was at the training ground at that time was regarded, by implication, as 'directly involved' in the coup, and arrested, including Sugiyah.

Under President Suharto's 'New Order', the publicity of the military rulers spread all kinds of stories of sex orgies at Lubang Buaya, and of atrocities committed by young girls; the purpose was 'to increase public hostility towards left-wing suspects and thus create the mood which prompted widespread reprisals and killings', as the AI report on Indonesia put it. 'It should be noted that, if the government's account of the Lubang Buaya incidents is

АССОЦИАЦИЯ СОВЕТСКИХ ЮРИСТОВ

ASSOCIATION DES JURISTES SOVIETIQUES

МОСКВА, К-9
ПРОСПЕКТ КАЛИНИНА, 14

14, AVENUE KALININE,
MOSCOU K-9
U.R.S.S.

" 27 " VII 1975 г.

№ _____

Mr. Martin Ennals
Secretary General of
Amnesty International

53, Theobald's Road
London WCIX 8SP

Dear Sir,

In connection with your letter dated April, 15 th and
so-called "Report of Conditions of Detention of Prisoniers of
Conscience" We would like to acknowlege you that ar we not eager
to discass about what you call a book and that is vulgar falsification and defamation on Soviet reality and socialist legeti-
macy.

Sincerely,   *L. Смирнов*.

L. Smirnov

President of the Soviet
Lawyer's Association

8. Photostat of a letter to AI from the Soviet Lawyers' Association

19. Major-General Grigorenko and his wife

20. Bulletin of the Baptist Church listing some of its arrested members in Soviet prisons (1973)

21. Pramoedya Ananta Toer, a historical
writer, permanently deprived of pencil
and paper in prison in Indonesia

22. Ugandan soldiers of the Simba battalion
with the corpses of Obote supporters in
1972, one year after Idi Amin had come
to power

23. Unknown Indonesian prisoners

AMNESTY

amnesty
international

1977 Prisoners of Conscience Year
World Campaign for Human Rights and against political repression and torture

Are Human Rights a Lost Cause?

"Every day, opening your paper in the morning, you read that somewhere in the world human beings are being thrown into prison, tortured or killed because their political or religious views are at variance with those of their government . . . . One experiences a feeling of unease and helplessness. Yet if disgust and disapproval could be translated into collective action, something effective might be done."

This statement is still terrifyingly relevant. It was made 15 years ago by a British lawyer, Peter Benenson, and Amnesty International was founded.

15 years prior to the making of this statement – that is, now 30 years ago – the Universal Declaration of Human Rights was adopted by the Plenary Session of the United Nations.

Now, three decades after the making of this Declaration, 15 years after Peter Benenson's appeal, let's examine the situation: millions of people have been persecuted; there have been countless victims of injustice and incredible cruelty, and still in many countries violent suppression of political opposition is the established procedure.

Is the fight for human rights really a lost cause?

THE GEOGRAPHY OF TERROR

We had intended to print a map of the world with black spots on it to indicate which countries are violating the Declaration of Human Rights. But we had to drop the idea as no map could possibly illustrate the actual gravity of the situation.

Amnesty International's 1975/76 Annual Report reveals that in just one year we have had to deal with human rights infringements in 112 countries. The Report states that there are more than 500,000 prisoners of conscience in the world and that torture is used in about 60 countries. Human rights are violated in every kind of country: members of the Eastern bloc, the Western bloc and the „Third World". The geography of political repression and torture is global.

To reduce the number of black terror spots on the map we must have more and more human rights campaigners all over the world.

Article 9 of the Universal Declaration of Human Rights: "No one shall be arbitrarily arrested, detained or exiled."

Can't Anything be Done to Help Prisoners of Conscience?

In our offices there are stacks of information and reports about innumerable cases of political oppression.

Human beings are degraded in every part of the world. They are subjected to:

– arbitrary imprisonment;
– unjust detention;
– the most modern and refined forms of torture;
– kidnapping;
– assassination.

All these crimes are committed over and over again.

And it is not only the actual political victims that we must consider, we must not forget their relatives (including children and friends who, although „free" are nevertheless in peril and suffering great distress.

They all need help, and every day Amnesty International shows how valuable it is to support and encourage these people.

Since Amnesty International was founded, thousands of our adopted prisoners of conscience have been freed. We have managed to help their families in all sorts of ways. We have also assisted numerous political refugees, and made life easier for them.

Persistent campaigning by our members all over the world has saved prisoners' lives and led to improved prison conditions for all categories of prisoners.

Moreover, the mobilization of public opinion everywhere against infringements of human rights has increased the speed and efficiency of our work.

The joint, practical, concentrated action proposed when Amnesty International was first founded is still our most effective means of guaranteeing basic human rights.

But to become increasingly efficient, our organization must grow. Our present membership is 100,000, and there must in addition be thousands who sympathize with our aims. All the same a tremendous amount of work and money is still needed for every prisoner we adopt and every victim of torture and oppression that we try to help.

So it is vital that we increase both our active membership and our funds. The success of our work is dependent on the devoted efforts of as many people as possible; and to remain solvent we must be able to rely on financial support from the general public.

We owe it to ourselves to do absolutely all we possibly can to help.

CALL TO ACTION!

We can all help provided we don't just give up but take action.

The number of victories won by Amnesty International over the torture and political persecution cases we have taken up reveal the effectiveness of direct, practical action.

Faced by the continuous violation of human rights we simply cannot remain silent.

We must take action to help prisoners of conscience and their families and to preserve civil liberties.

You can take action through Amnesty International. Read the facts and decide what you are going to do about the situation.

24. Amnesty International's main medium of information for its English-reading members and supporters

SINGAPORE

Journalist internerad i 12 år utan rättegång

25. National AI sections produce campaign material in their own languages

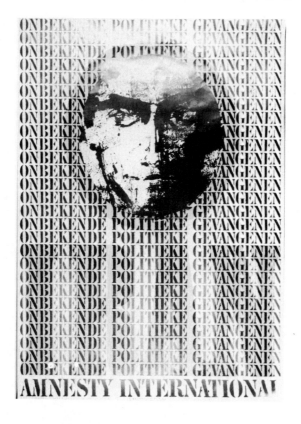

26. David Simpson, Director and Press Officer of AI's British section

27. Amnesty's work is never done: two months after General Franco's demise, Spanish riot police still attack demonstrators (Barcelona, February 1976)

28. Steve Biko, died while detained incommunicado by South African police in 1977

29. Oryol prison hospital, USSR

30. Thomas Hammerberg (Sweden) receives the Nobel Peace Prize for Amnesty International in December 1977

true, nonetheless the government has never attempted to prove this by putting the Lubang Buaya girl prisoners on trial. In eleven years, an estimated eight hundred prisoners have been brought to court — but not a single girl who was at Lubang Buaya. The reluctance of the government to establish the truth of the Lubang Buaya allegations in the courts has been Amnesty International's main reason for deciding to take up the cases of girl prisoners such as Sugiyah.'

At the other end of the age scale of women prisoners is Charlotte Salawati, known and respected in Indonesia as 'Ibu' (mother) Salawati, born in 1909. She was a long-standing AI adoption case; after ten years of detention without trial, she was released in 1976. She had been prominent in the nationalist movement which won Indonesia's independence from Dutch colonial rule, sat for the Communist Party in parliament and was a Deputy Chairwoman of the leading women's association *Gerwani*. However, she had always retained the Christian beliefs in which she had been brought up. She was a member of the official Indonesian delegation to the Peace Congress in Helsinki in 1965, shortly before her arrest. There was no evidence against her. The authorities obviously never intended to bring her to trial. Nor did they given any explanation when she was released.

Gerwani was a legal organization until after the coup of 1965, but many of its members were immediately arrested. Others escaped by moving to other areas, and some were able to buy their freedom — the military officers running the prisons often offered to release detainees for money (usually something like 50,000 rupiahs per head). Great numbers of trade union activists among the women workers were also arrested after dismissal from their jobs. Other women were picked up at random in the streets and sent to prison when they were unable to identify themselves. Mothers of sons or daughters sought by the army were arrested; or women were simply taken away with their husbands or brothers just because they were relatives.

A London Sunday paper published, in 1976, an interview with a girl who had been a member of a left-wing organization as a teenager. Three years after the 1965 coup she was arrested and tortured at the local military post: she was stripped naked, beaten by an 'intelligence' officer, her pubic and head hair was burnt, and she was put on a table where a stick was inserted in her vagina. She was also forced to watch the torture of other woman prisoners.

'It is not possible to establish precisely how many women are still being held without trial,' says the 1977 AI report on Indonesia.

'There are women's prisons throughout the archipelago. Probably about two thousand women are being held without trial.'

Perhaps the most disturbing recent developments are the large-scale arrests of Muslims, students, and other ethnic minorities in 1977 and 1978. Following widespread student unrest over the alleged corruption in the government and the unopposed re-election of President Suharto, the government arrested large numbers of students in February and March 1978. This was followed in April 1978 by a second wave of arrests of prominent Muslim figures. Supporters of the official Muslim party, the *Partai Persatuan Pembangunan* (PPP), have suffered particularly. Since 1965 the PPP has emerged as the major focus of opposition to the military government.

Dictatorships, whatever their political hue, are not the kind of governmental system to which wisdom comes as a gift of nature. What the Indian poet and journalist Dom Moraes wrote in 1972 after a visit to the island of Buru could, with a few alterations, apply just as well to the situation in some East European countries:

'It was stupid, in 1965, to decide that a mass of small, helpless people, clerks and bank tellers and office workers, were all hardline Communists; stupid to decide that several of the leading intellectuals of the country were hardline Communists without any trial or investigation whatever. It is stupid to have kept them locked up for six years, unable to communicate with their families, and eventually committed them to Buru, two thousand miles from their homes. It is stupid to try and turn intellectuals into manual labourers.'

Black Hero or Insane Murderer?

Among the countries of the Third World which have, on and off, enjoyed Moscow's friendship, Uganda is certainly the most problematic one. But it would be a mistake to regard it as East Africa's trouble spot only since Idi Amin usurped power. In its report for 1966-67, AI stated that the country held 'by far the largest number of political prisoners' in the area. President Obote, a former salesman in Kenya, had become Uganda's ruler, with the help of Britain's somewhat misguided sponsorship, in 1962. Four years later, he assumed what amounted to dictatorial powers. Amnesty took up the cases of several political prisoners in Uganda, including those of five ministers arrested when Obote suspended the constitution, and of a number of well-known people imprisoned when he overthrew and arrested the Kabaka of Buganda — Uganda's most important kingdom. Amnesty adopted over thirty cases, and discussed the situation with Obote and his Foreign Minister in Kampala and London; it was, however, difficult to check whether their promises were kept, as arrests and releases alternated rapidly. But one thing was certain, Obote's prominent political prisoners were systematically ill-treated to make them confess to plots against the regime. Many, including AI adoptees, were kept for months in solitary confinement in punishment cells. Their physical condition deteriorated — one went mad. Amnesty took up the issue with the Organization of African Unity (OAU), the Red Cross, and other international bodies.

It was no great surprise to observers of the African scene when an army coup deposed Obote in January, 1971, exiling him from Uganda. The coup leader was a self-styled general, Idi Amin, whose main military experience had been his training at Sandhurst as a cook. He released at once more than fifty people held under Obote's emergency regulations, several of them Amnesty cases. A month after the coup, John Humphreys, who ran AI's African research department, visited Kampala to review the situation.

It soon became clear that Uganda had been pushed out of the frying pan into the fire by Amin. He abolished parliament, suspended political activities, and assumed his one-man rule by decree. Security forces were given wide powers of arrest and detention. But much worse was to come as he consolidated his position during the following years. Decree followed decree. Military tribunals were empowered by President Amin to try civilians for capital charges such as sedition and treason, and for new offences like 'acts calculated to intimidate or alarm members of the public or bring the military under contempt or into disrepute'. Military tribunals were also to try 'economic crimes', now made capital offences, from overcharging to hoarding and embezzlement. All Asian settlers, most of them traders, were expelled and their businesses confiscated. In February, 1973, there were twelve public executions by firing squads — no figures were given for other 'legal' executions since 1971.

But many illegal ones, in other words murders carried out on Amin's orders, or at least with his approval, became common knowledge in Uganda and the outside world. In 1972, the Chief Justice, Benedicto Kiwanuka, was dragged from the court chambers, taken away in an army car, and murdered, apparently because he had demanded the independence of the judiciary. A businessman who had been acquitted against the wishes of the police was shot dead in the street; his lawyer was arrested and severely tortured. A number of Ugandans, arrested for alleged political offences, just 'disappeared'; so did two Americans, some foreign girl students, one or two of Amin's discarded wives, and several witnesses who might have revealed the truth about police killings. Some security officers were tried by a military tribunal in connection with eighteen cases of 'disappearances', but all were acquitted. Numerous killings of Ugandans followed the Israeli raid on Entebbe in July, 1976, which freed the hostages from a hijacked airliner — except an elderly British-Israeli lady, Mrs. Dora Bloch who, according to witnesses, was strangled after being taken from hospital by security officers. The Ugandan photographer who was said to have taken a picture of the dead woman was also killed.

Amnesty collected as much evidence as possible, but witnesses who were prepared to talk were few: fear stalks Uganda, and even refugees who found asylum in Kenya were afraid for their friends and relatives still within Amin's reach. Nevertheless, it became clear that security forces usually made victims 'disappear' by bundling them at gunpoint into the backs, or boots, of their vehicles, taking them to isolated places in the bush, and killing them with considerable brutality. 'Mass killings have taken place within the army, numbering thousands of deaths, in 1971-1972 and 1974,' AI stated in a Submission to the U.N. Commission on Human Rights (1977). 'Large numbers of prominent civilians (lawyers, academics, religious leaders, civil servants, doctors, former politicians, journalists, sportsmen etc.) have been arrested and subsequently "disappeared".'

Torture after arrest is almost routine. Two Kenyans described what happened to them at Nakuru prison in March, 1976:

'The police boss, even without demanding our documents, ordered that we be taken into custody and that we be whipped twenty strokes each. In the cells we found a truck wheel-rim. We were ordered to kneel down, put our heads through the ring, and stay in that position until the whipping ended. Any movement, we were warned, would be tantamount to demanding more punishment, like "being sent to the moon", which we later understood to mean we would be shot.'

Another victim described his experience during interrogation. The guard was ordered to 'give him what he has come here for': forty lashes.

'Then I was held down with soldiers treading on my wrists and legs, and pins were stuck under my toenails . . . . The next day we were ordered to crawl over some very sharp stones which cut our knees and hands till they bled. The two in front were ordered to go outside. I heard two shots and then four of us were ordered to go outside too. I thought this was the end, but we were just told to load the bodies into a landrover.'

Prisoners were not only forced to remove the bodies of their murdered fellow-prisoners — they were frequently made to do the killing themselves, often with car axles or sledge hammers; the survivors were then shot. There were also allegations of mutilation, rape, sexual torture, and the more sophisticated electric tortures carried out by 'State Research Units'.

AI tried several times to verify the accusations made against Amin and his subordinates. In 1975, there seemed to be a chance to question him personally when he invited an Amnesty mission to a press conference at the United Nations. But then AI was informed that the time was 'not suitable', after all; no alternative date was offered. Meanwhile, the estimates of total killings in Uganda were mounting year after year; according to AI's *Human Rights Violations in Uganda*, published in the spring of 1978, the figure was 'anywhere around 300,000 or above' since Amin's rise to power. Reliable reports said that over 200 hundred Kenyans living in Uganda had been murdered in a 'systematic and indiscriminate massacre' in July, 1976.

In January of the following year, AI used the sixth anniversary of his assumption to power to send a cable to 'President Idi Amin Dada', as he liked to be called, repeating its offer to undertake a fact-finding mission to Uganda. There was no reply. Three weeks later, Amnesty sent another cable to Amin, expressing serious doubts about official explanations for the deaths of Archbishop Dr. Janani Luwum and government ministers Oboth-Ofumbi and Lieutenant-Colonel Oryema. They were officially reported to have been killed in a car accident on February 16 — after their public denunciation and arrest on treason charges. These 'accidental' deaths happened one week after reports of widespread arrests, and two weeks after AI had called on the U.N. Human Rights Commission to launch an urgent international enquiry into gross violations of human rights in Uganda.

Amin's deeds were no laughing matter, yet in Europe he had become a laughing-stock and one of the cartoonists' favourite subjects because of his frequent absurd utterances and exhibitionist antics in his role as the leader of a Commonwealth country. Doctors who had treated him said that he was suffering from syphilis and seemed to have entered the tertiary stage, affecting the brain. Strangely enough, however, his grandiloquent attacks on Britain and his deliberate humiliation of white people in Uganda endeared him to a good many Africans; they may have liked his favourite means of transport at public celebrations — to be carried on a throne by Europeans. At least one of the throne-bearers, a British settler, subsequently 'disappeared'. The fact that Amin also killed many thousands of his own black subjects, preferably those of other tribes and religions than his own, did not seem to have eliminated the open or sneaking admiration of that black hero. It is mainly in neighbouring Kenya and Tanzania that Amin has always been generally regarded as what the outside world had come to call him: an insane murderer.

4

The Death Penalty: Judicial Murder or Deterrent?

Violence in the 1970s
Amnesty celebrated its tenth anniversary, and the phenomenal rise of the scope and success of its activities, in 1971. There were now well over a thousand groups in thirty-one countries, seven hundred and twenty-seven adopted prisoners had been released within the calendar year, and the annual budget surpassed £100,000. Most important of all, the growth of the movement showed no signs of slackening.

But there was little cause for rejoicing, to say nothing of relaxing; for one major factor contributing to the world-wide interest in Amnesty's cause was the equally world-wide and horrifying flare-up of violence which had marked the preceding years: the Arab-Israeli war of 1967, the Soviet invasion of Czechoslovakia of 1968, the intensifying war in Vietnam, the right-wing coups in Latin America, the new troubles in Northern Ireland.

In the old days, the treatment of captured soldiers was the concern of the International Red Cross. Now, the borderline between soldiers and civilians, between military and anarchic violence was disappearing — with the unfortunate and unarmed denizens as the victims. Terrorists, hi-jackers, kidnappers, assassins appeared in increasing numbers as self-styled 'soldiers' for this or that cause — from the liberation of Ulster to that of Palestine. In Vietnam, whole villages were wiped out as the SS had wiped out Lidice, and according to information collected by AI no less than 100,000 civilian detainees were being held by the Saigon regime. In 1972, the British government accepted a minority report on brutal interrogation methods used by security forces in Ulster. At the Olympic Games in Munich, Arab terrorists caused a bloodbath among Israeli sportsmen. An AI delegate to South Korea reported that dozens of opponents to the regime had been made to confess under torture, and the honorary president of the South Korean Amnesty section, a bishop, was sentenced to fifteen years' imprisonment for alleged financial help to dissidents.

In those years, the number of death sentences and executions was rising alarmingly — in Spain, Indonesia, South America, South Korea, the Soviet Union, Iran, China, Bulgaria, the German Democratic Republic. The guillotine was used again in France, and, in the USA, pressure was mounting for again carrying out the death penalty, after ten years of no executions. Not all the victims were alleged political offenders, but Amnesty International was increasingly concerned about the whole issue of capital punishment.

The abolition of the death penalty for political prisoners had been one of AI's interests right from the start, but it had not been emphasized as a cause to which every member was supposed to subscribe, except where prisoners of conscience were involved. The reason was obvious: the whole movement was geared to help these prisoners, not people convicted for murder and other violent acts. But there was also another reason: during AI's first years of consolidation, its activities had to be concentrated on help for political prisoners, and it would have been unwise to put off potential new members by focussing on such a controversial cause as the general abolition of the death penalty.

It was at the meeting of the AI International Council in Vienna in 1973 — opened by the Austrian Chancellor, Dr. Bruno Kreisky — that AI reaffirmed the movement's stand against capital punishment, and for its world-wide abolition. A group of parliamentarians from seven Council of Europe countries had already submitted a motion to this effect to its Consultative Assembly, and a request was cabled to the UN Economic and Social Council, urging all UN members to abolish capital punishment as a legal sanction. AI's basic position was made clear: that the death penalty 'must now be seen as a violation of the human right not to be subjected to torture and cruel, inhuman or degrading treatment'.

A year after Vienna, the AI International Council met in Askov in Denmark. This was the meeting at which Sean MacBride announced his resignation as chairman of the International Executive, a month before he was awarded the Nobel Peace Prize 'in recognition of his lifelong work for human rights'. Dirk Börner of the German Federal Republic was elected as the new chairman, and for the first time an ex-prisoner of conscience, Mümtaz Soysal of

Turkey, was elected to the Executive of AI, now enlarged from seven to nine members. At the Askov meeting, the AI statute was rephrased, defining the three central aims as help for prisoners of conscience, campaign against torture, and campaign for the abolition of capital punishment — all three issues of equal importance.

However, another four years went by until AI's great attack on the death penalty, still retained in over 100 countries, was furnished with a fundamental propaganda weapon, a 125,000-word document. This 'Death Penalty Report', to be published in 1979, was compiled by the Research Department, the legal office, and by a young British barrister, Brian Wrobel. He had begun his work for AI on a mission to South Korea as a trial observer in 1975, when eight members of the People's Revolutionary Party were sentenced to death for 'anti-state activities'. The defence lawyers had been kept under house arrest at one stage, thus being unable to help the prisoners; Wrobel himself was manhandled by the police one day when trying to enter the court. The sentenced prisoners were allowed no time to appeal, or to petition the President of South Korea for clemency. They were at once executed by hanging.

'The case illustrates dramatically that defendants in South Korea have grossly inadequate opportunity to present a defence, and that in this case justice was neither done nor seen to be done,' wrote Wrobel in his report for AI. He had always been opposed to capital punishment, but this traumatic experience confirmed him as an abolitionist.

Amnesty's files of the 1970s were full of reports of killings, with and without court sentences, from all over the world. From July, 1974, to April, 1976, AI catalogued three hundred and seventy-nine cases of deaths and disappearances under the then new president of Guatemala, Kjell Laugerud — all believed to have been 'extrajudicial executions'. AI called on President Alfredo Stroessner of Paraguay in 1976 to explain the deaths of a number of people at the hands of the police — five of them reportedly under torture. Two peasant leaders were decapitated in front of their wives and children, and one of the wives was subsequently arrested and lost her reason — like the other five hundred to eight hundred Paraguayan political prisoners who also went mad as a result of torture. One British subject, the lecturer Denis Hills, was sentenced to death in Uganda but freed when Foreign Secretary Callaghan flew from London to Kampala to plead for the man's life.

AI had also pleaded for the lives of the two dozen or more people executed at Kunming in south-western China in a new series of killings in various parts of the country in the spring of 1977. They were accused of 'political crimes' in connection with the so-called Gang of Four, led by Mao's widow. Local radio broadcasts kept reporting death sentences and executions by firing squads in twelve widely separated towns after posters had appeared on the walls: the usual way of announcing court sentences. During one weekend, such posters listing ten people sentenced to death were seen in Peking, and 26 names of executed 'counter-revolutionaries' in Shanghai in 1977.

Eduard Kuznetsov, a Leningrad Jew imprisoned several times, recalled in his *Prison Diaries* (published in an English translation in London, 1975) that in the Mordovian penal colony where he spent seven years 'dozens of prisoners were executed for tattooing anti-government slogans on their bodies or for self-mutilations of various kinds'.

In the autumn of 1977, the Duvalier family celebrated the twentieth anniversary of their dictatorship on Haiti, while in Paris AI held a meeting of members of groups from all over Europe who had adopted Haitian political prisoners. Some of the about one hundred prisoners released to mark the anniversary were also in Paris to tell their tale. Three thousand citizens of that 'island in the sun' (total population: c. 9 million) had been killed in twenty years. When François ('Papa Doc') Duvalier died in 1971, his son Jean-Claude ('Bébé Doc') took over and had two hundred political detainees executed in Fort Dimanche Prison, Port-au-Prince. Torture and death, the AI meeting was told, were still daily occurrences in Haiti, whose president denied that there were any political prisoners at all. But the exiles knew the names of one hundred and seventy-six who had died in Fort Dimanche during the previous two years, among them a former Minister of Justice. Most of them died of tuberculosis, malaria, or typhoid, some starved to death. The ex-prisoners described one ghastly scene some of them had to watch — a dying prisoner being eaten by worms. Others were forced to lick the victims' blood off the floors of torture chambers. No wonder many prisoners went insane under these conditions which AI denounced as 'among the most inhumane in the world'.

The Haiti tragedy raised the basic question: would the world-wide official abolition of capital punishment make the slightest difference in a dictatorship? Few of the Duvaliers' victims had been sentenced to death. Such legal formalities are simply not needed by a tyrannical regime.

The Death Penalty Around the World

Amnesty's statute has always committed the movement to 'opposing, by all appropriate means, the imposition of death penalties' because some lives could be saved by abolition, at least in countries where ordinary, open courts are functioning according to democratic constitutions and laws. AI's basic attitude is that capital punishment is 'cruel, inhuman and degrading' within the meaning of Article 5 of the United Nations Declaration of Human Rights. The movement's opposition to it rests on the grounds that it is 'irrevocable, is capable of being inflicted on the innocent, does not act as a deterrent to crime, and is a violation of the right to life provisions' laid down in the U.N. Declaration and other international covenants. It is, of course, an attitude deviating from AI's general principle of concerning itself mainly with helping those prisoners of conscience who have not committed or advocated violence. There is, therefore, the logical argument that the abolition of the death penalty would benefit people who have used violence, namely murderers, and it has done so in those countries which have already done away with capital punishment.

This is not only an objection voiced by some Amnesty supporters; it is also one of the most formidable obstacles to creating, in our age of violence, the climate of public opinion for abolition in countries which still execute convicted murderers. However, the guideline for AI activities adopted by the International Executive Council in July, 1977, deals in the first place with individual death penalty cases: 'In principle, actions should be undertaken for prisoners whether or not they are prisoners of conscience'; but where it is not practicable to take up all cases that come to the attention of AI, 'actions may be taken according to the importance within the general context of efforts to promote abolition'.

What does this mean in terms of everyday practice of the International Secretariat, the national sections and the adoption groups? AI makes the point that a high priority should be given to individual cases of prisoners of conscience sentenced to death, and suggests how this may be put into practice by these guidelines:

'The cases should be selected in a way that they represent "legal key-cases". Our approach here should focus on the general principles and not so much on the individual case itself . . . . We are not defending murderers − we are working against the death penalty. This approach necessitates case-to-case decisions. The International Secretariat should be entitled to take these decisions, and in doubt it could seek advice from the Executive member

107

responsible . . . . Our traditional work for the release of prisoners of conscience should not be downgraded to give room for the death-penalty
activities. A balance should be maintained. Urgent action campaigns should
be the main machinery for individual death-penalty cases. National sections
should be encouraged to form anti-death penalty urgent-action groups.'

If one looks at the world map, trying to assess the general attitude of countries to abolition or retention, the picture does not
seem too encouraging for the abolitionists. Only six European
countries have done away altogether with capital punishment:
Sweden, Portugal, Austria, Finland, Iceland and the German Federal
Republic — but in the latter country, terrorist activities have recently created a perceptible climate in favour of the re-introduction
of the death penalty. Four more countries have abolished it only
for peacetime offences, preserving it for specified crimes — Britain,
for instance, for treason, though no one has been sentenced to
death for this for a long time. Here, capital punishment for murder
was abolished in 1965 for a trial period of five years and never reintroduced after 1970. In the Republic of Ireland, there have been
no executions since 1954. In most other West European countries,
death sentences have been commuted almost automatically,
though in France two persons were executed in recent years despite
a widespread and vociferous movement in favour of abolition. In
Cyprus, three people were executed in 1962. In Switzerland, which
had abolished the death penalty in 1874, a public opinion poll held
in 1978 produced a two-thirds majority for reintroducing it in
cases where terrorists have taken human lives.

So long as Franco ruled Spain, executions — and, of course,
extra-judicial killings — were carried out frequently; the deaths by
garotting of eleven alleged terrorists in 1975 shook the civilized
world. Three years later, the Spanish government prepared a bill to
replace capital punishment, which was still in force after Franco's
death, by up to forty years' imprisonment; these sentences could
not be wiped out by pardons or amnesties. In Eastern Europe, the
Communist countries are all committed, by the principles of
Socialist legal theory, to eventual abolition, but the practice is still
a long way off. In the Soviet Union, some of the 30 or more people
sentenced to death each year from 1974 to 1976 had been convicted merely of 'theft of state property' or similar 'economic
crimes'. In some of the republics of the USSR there is no right of
appeal at all.

Reliable information about death sentences and executions in the Middle East is difficult to obtain, but one knows that in those countries where justice is administered under Islamic law — Saudi Arabia, Oman, Libya, the Yemen Arab Republic — not only murder but also certain sex offences are subject to the death penalty. Traditionally, adultery between two married people is punished by stoning both the man and the woman to death; one case in Saudi Arabia known to AI took place in 1977 when three married men were killed in this way, and a princess who had secretly married a commoner in 1978 was shot while the man was beheaded. So were two Saudis convicted of indecently assaulting a boy. Laws based on the Koran are very severe; in Libya, the hand of a convicted thief is hacked off. In the Yemen, 70 alleged saboteurs were executed between May and December of 1973.

'The general acceptance in the Middle East of the death penalty,' says AI, 'is a result of the deeply embedded Islamic tradition and customary practice.' It is therefore unlikely that a move towards the total abolition of capital punishment in any of the Middle Eastern countries will take place in the near future. The exception, of course, is Israel as a non-Islamic country; here, the only case of execution has so far been that of the Nazi leader Adolf Eichmann for genocide.

Most African countries, the independent black ones as well as those under white minority rule, have legal provisions for the use of capital punishment; however, the frequency with which it is imposed and inflicted varies considerably from country to country. At one extreme there are the dictatorial regimes and police states — like Uganda and South Africa — which have a complete disregard for their own constitutions when it comes to getting rid of some *persona non grata*, or even making a massacre of whole groups of people. As a rule, no formal court sentences are necessary so long as the army and the police function as executioners. At the other end there are some new governments, such as the Frelimo administration in Mozambique, which have officially adopted abolition as their eventual aim. Other states, among them the Malagasy Republic and Ghana, still have the death penalty, but have invariably granted commution by executive clemency in recent years.

The white minority regime in Rhodesia has attempted to use capital punishment as a means of intimidating its black population into betraying the activities of nationalist guerillas; judicial amendments in the 1970s made it a capital offence even to provide food and/or shelter to insurgents, or to fail to report their presence to the security forces. Many executions on these grounds have taken place. Nigeria and Ethiopia, grappling with the aftermath of rebellions and civil wars, re-introduced public executions, and after an abortive coup in the Sudan in 1976, nearly a hundred people were shot. Zambia and Kenya introduced mandatory capital punishment for armed robbery in the mid-1970s. Ethiopia and Uganda decreed it also for 'economic offences'. Of course, murders of political opponents and whole population groups, when carried out by these governments themselves, are tacitly permitted.

Many Latin-American countries, however, abolished the death penalty in the nineteenth and early twentieth centuries. Ecuador, for instance, turned abolitionist as far back as 1852, Venezuela soon afterwards, and Costa Rica and Uruguay at the end of the last century. The Venezuelan constitution of 1961 is very outspoken: 'The right to life is inviolable. No law may establish the death penalty, nor any authority carry it out.' In only three Latin-American countries — El Salvador, Haiti, and Peru — the death penalty is enshrined in the constitution, especially for high treason, crimes against state security, and murder. Some other countries, such as Mexico, Guatemala, and Nicaragua, have made certain legal provisions for imposing death sentences in the cases of particularly cruel crimes. Argentina, Bolivia, Brazil, and Chile have re-introduced the death penalty following military coups in the 1960s and 1970s. In Cuba, there were many summary executions after the Castro revolution of 1959, and Haiti under Duvalier declared 'Communist activities of any kind' as punishable by death.

'The comparatively positive picture presented by the judicial aspect of the death penalty issue in Latin America,' reported AI, 'is countered by the dark reality of officially sanctioned political murder practised in several countries. Para-military groups which are condoned by, or act in cooperation with government forces operate particularly in Argentina and Guatemala. The *Ley de Fuga*, whereby a prisoner is shot on the pretext of attempted escape, has been applied to political prisoners in Argentina and Chile . . . . Deaths under torture and so-called "disappearances" or unrecognized arrests also occur in the Dominican Republic, Haiti, Nicaragua, Paraguay and Uruguay.'

What this abhorrent scene teaches is the lesson that the legal and constitutional abolition of capital punishment has no practical value if a new set of rulers decides that executions, with or without court sentence, is what they need to keep themselves in power. They simply re-introduce the death penalty, or they just carry it out without bothering about judicial sanction.

110

In the more firmly established democracies of the Americas, abolition really means the end of capital punishment. After intense public discussion, Canada finally abolished it for civilian crimes in 1976. In the USA, courts at State as well as Federal level were given the opportunity to decide whether it constitutes 'cruel and unusual punishment' within the meaning of the 8th and 14th Amendments to the Constitution. In several States, legislatures have debated not only the general issues involved, but also the methods employed in judicial killing, and in 1976 the US Supreme Court decided that the death penalty is not *per se* a 'cruel and unusual punishment'. Anyway, only seventeen States have abolished it, while thirty-three States have retained it — though there was only one execution in the decade from 1967 to 1977.

In the Caribbean islands which are members of the British Commonwealth, jurisdiction is based on English common law; mandatory death sentence has been retained for murder and in some cases for piracy, but there have been only a few executions. For all these territories, except Guyana, the Privy Council in London is the final court of appeal, and in most of them death sentences may be commuted by the Crown.

In every Asian country, states AI, the death penalty exists and is being mercilessly carried out, except in the Crown Colony Hong Kong, where all death sentences have been commuted to life imprisonment since 1966. Many Far Eastern countries have recently extended capital punishment to cover drug trafficking; in Singapore, the mere possession of more than two grammes of heroin is punished by death. In Thailand, where King Bhumibol has promulgated no fewer than five constitutions within four years, the Prime Minister has been given the absolute right to order executions for drug offences. Pakistan and Bangladesh are also among the countries which have put additional offences under the threat of capital punishment. In Sri Lanka, it was suspended in 1956; an official commission came to the conclusion that it 'did not have a deterrent effect in cases of homicide'. And it was re-introduced in 1959; ever since there have been widespread demands that it should be finally abolished. Nepal did this as long ago as 1931 for ordinary crimes, but there were two recent death sentences for an attempt on the life of the King and for treason; however they were not carried out.

Japan conducted an official poll in 1975 to gauge public opinion on capital punishment; 57% of those questioned were against abolition. But in 1978, the Japanese parliament extended the death penalty in an act of tough new legislation to cases of hijacking and the seizure of diplomatic establishments, while raising from five years to life imprisonment the penalty for members of armed gangs who take hostages. In India, however, where dozens of people are executed every year for ordinary crimes, there is considerable public debate on the question of abolition. Indian lawyers and campaigners for civil liberty are in favour of abolishing the death penalty, but in 1967 a Report of the Law Commission declared itself for retention with an argument which does not sound very convincing: hanging should continue because of 'the conditions of India, the variety of the social upbringing of its inhabitants, the disparity of the level of morality and education in the country, the vastness of its area, the diversity of its population and the paramount need for maintaining law and order in the country at the present juncture.'

For and Against Capital Punishment

Is the death penalty judicial murder, or does it act as a deterrent? This is a fundamental question which has been submitted to general public opinion and which still troubles most people. The 1978 AI Report lists the arguments for and against abolition.

Capital punishment is a unique deterrent, say the retentionists. It is more effective than protracted imprisonment or other alternative forms of severe punishment, and based on the 'self-evident truth' that man wants to preserve his life. Capital punishment emphasizes the gravity of murder, increases the community's abhorrence of this crime, and will thus decrease the incidence of murder in the long run.

The anti-abolitionists also point out that there is little risk of executing innocent people; in all countries with a well-established judicial system, each murder charge is heard in two or three courts, and proof 'beyond any reasonable doubt' is required for conviction. The question of reprieve is carefully considered. The accused's fitness to plead must be established; his defence of insanity is available, and a killer who may have been of unsound mind when he committed the deed is unlikely to be executed. There is no satisfactory alternative to capital punishment; life-long imprisonment may well be more cruel than execution. On the other hand, a murderer released from prison may kill again.

'A life for a life' is a demand that appeals to man's innate sense of justice: the punishment should fit the crime of those who have deliberately violated the sanctity of human life. Although the abolition of the death penalty may do no harm in advanced western countries, the circumstances in the Third World are so different that the western experience is irrelevant. In those developing countries, the threat of execution is a more effective deterrent than that of prolonged imprisonment which, in most cases, means that the murderer will be better off than in his own home.

Public opinion, say the retentionists, is overwhelmingly in favour of capital punishment, and it would be dangerous for the law in Third World countries to move too far ahead of people's attitudes. Abolition would go against the opinions of many judges, lawyers and police officers with wide experience of crime, who all favour the retention of the death penalty.

The arguments of the abolitionists are these: Capital punishment is not an effective deterrent. One cannot assume that all potential murderers calculate the difference between execution and prolonged imprisonment — the murderer, if he plans his deed carefully, is mainly concerned with avoiding detection while the murderer who acts in the heat of passion does not calculate anything at all. However, the greatest deterrent is fear of capture and arrest, irrespective of the consequences.

Psychopaths have been known to confess falsely to unsolved murders in order to attract the sentence of death, to be executed, and thereby avoid the need for suicide. In none of the countries which have suspended or abolished capital punishment — in the western or in the Third World — has there been a resulting increase in the murder rate; in some of these countries, for instance in the abolitionist States of the USA and Australia, incidences of murder have remained virtually the same. In the long run, the abolition of capital punishment, by reaffirming the state's reverence for human life, may influence the minds of its citizens, thus decreasing the incidence of murder in the community.

The argument that innocent people are hardly ever convicted of capital crimes is contradicted by the numerous cases in which this has happened. Also, the present legal definition of insanity often appears too narrow, and in the Third World psychiatric services may be inadequate to save insane killers from execution.

Murder trials, with the gallows looming at their end, tend to be protracted and sensational; public attention is focussed on the undesirable aspects of human behaviour, and the administration of justice is distorted by making the dispassionate examination of the evidence more difficult. Statistics and experience show that the risk of a murderer killing again after release from prison is no greater than the relapse of a man imprisoned for other crimes, such as armed robbery or causing grievous bodily harm, which do not carry the death penalty.

The emotional argument of 'a life for a life' does not morally entitle the state to kill people. Capital punishment, being judicial murder, denies the sanctity of life, which is an essential value for the state to support; the disregard of this value tends to lower respect for life in the public mind.

Conviction and sentencing of all crimes, including those carrying the death sentence, often depend on the efficiency of counsel for prosecution and defence, the personalities and attitudes of the judges and the jurors. Defence lawyers may, or may not, succeed in obtaining retrials and saving their clients from execution on various grounds which often have little to do with his guilt or innocence. In the famous case of Caryl Chessman, an American who claimed he was innocent of the charge which resulted in his being condemned to death, they used every method known to the law for obtaining a retrial; counsel managed to prolong his life on Death Row, San Quentin, for twelve years, but they failed ultimately, and he was executed in 1960.

Abolitionists quote what Chessman wrote (in *Trial by Ordeal*) about the condemned prisoners' sufferings before their execution:

> 'I've witnessed the disintegration of the minds of the men around me. I've seen those men naked on the floor, rolling in their own excrement. I've listened as they smashed and shattered the sinks and toilets and fixtures in their cells. I've watched them savagely attack one another. I've heard their prayers and their screams and their curses. I've observed their bodies being removed after they had destroyed themselves. I've read their pathetic pleas for mercy . . . .'

Execution, say the opponents of capital punishment, may not result in a quick death. In the case of hanging, it may come by slow strangulation if the calculations for the length of the drop have been made incorrectly. Electrocution may result in burning flesh before the heart stops beating. In the gas chamber, observers have seen evidence of painful asphyxiation, with the eyes of the prisoner turning purple and bulging from their sockets. The garotte, Spain's traditional method of execution, is designed to kill a man by breaking his neck, but often he is strangulated to death. The guillotine, as used in France, may be the most 'humane' way of killing, but beheading by axe has often needed more than one stroke for severing the head, depending on the skill of the executioner, or the lack of it. Death by intravenous lethal injection works quickly only if the victim holds absolutely still; its speed may also depend on the thickness of the fat layer covering the veins.

These are the main arguments of the abolitionists, but there are many others, often based on religious attitudes such as the Bible word, 'Vengeance is mine; I will repay, saith the Lord' (Romans, 12:19).

The arguments of those who want to retain or re-introduce the death penalty have recently been extended by the increase of terrorist violence and by the cases in which such prisoners have managed to escape, or been released by their comrades' blackmail, only to carry out more acts of violence.

In December, 1977, two hundred AI delegates from fifty countries met in Stockholm to discuss the movement's fight against capital punishment. The conference ended with the launching of an appeal to the United Nations to outlaw the death penalty, still being retained by over a hundred countries, and to condemn extrajudicial executions as a form of political coercion.

Amnesty International has a difficult task in trying to swing global public opinion towards condemnation of capital punishment. However, the movement's basic campaign for the release of prisoners of conscience has never been easy either, yet it has had, over the years, an astonishing measure of success, mainly due to the deep conviction of AI members that innocent people, who have not used or advocated violence, are being wronged and must be helped. The campaign against the death penalty, on the other hand, must also deal with men and women who have been found guilty of abhorrent crimes, and who have used violence. There are Amnesty supporters who believe that at a time when crimes against society are on the increase, society has the right to use capital punishment in self-defence. Amnesty may have to face its most serious crisis yet.

5

Amnesty Ennobled

A Case History

Josefina A., an arts student in Buenos Aires in her mid-twenties who was expecting a baby, had disappeared. Her family asked a friend, an Amnesty supporter, for help. He informed AI's International Secretariat in London, and a South American journalist in England was asked for his assistance. He enquired about the case during one of his regular telephone calls to Buenos Aires, and was soon able to report back to AI: 'Josefina has been arrested. Her family has been trying to trace her by filing writs of *habeas corpus*, but they got no official answer.'

The International Secretariat referred the case to the Americas Division of the Research Department which occupies, with its sixty workers, three floors of the movement's headquarters in a tall old office building near London's Strand. The Research Department is responsible for collecting and analyzing information on violations of human rights anywhere in the world, and especially for keeping comprehensive records on prisoners of conscience. There is also a Documentation Centre for the storage and retrieval of information; it maintains a special library on political imprisonment.

All this may sound somewhat bureaucratic and over-organized, but the system has been developed on the basis of AI's experience over the years. There are a good many pitfalls, legal and political, which have to be avoided; AI simply cannot afford to act on unchecked information which might prove unreliable — it is human life and freedom that are at stake. So the Research Department must be able to evaluate information about arrests, detention, trials and conditions in any country in the light of legal, social, and

116

political developments, and to provide the fullest possible details about the country's living conditions as well as about individual prisoners.

There is no national section in Argentina; most countries ruled by dictators or juntas have no such organized AI branches, only individual members and also 'contacts' who are often in danger of being themselves made into prisoners of conscience. In Josefina's case, such an Amnesty member provided the link with London. But information may reach the International Secretariat from all kinds of sources: newspapers and journals in dozens of languages, visits from relatives of prisoners and exiles, letters from the prisoners themselves — sometimes smuggled out of prison; news about arrests may come from lawyers, churches, professional organizations, trade unions, resistance groups, or AI's own fact-finding missions. Whatever that information is, it must be carefully studied, checked and cross-checked before any action is taken. In particular, AI must be absolutely sure that the prisoner has not used or advocated violence. Josefina was 'cleared' as suitable for adoption.

Two months after her arrest, her family was told that she was being held in Villa Devoto, a women's prison in Buenos Aires. There was no charge against her, nor was there any reason given for her arrest. However, she had once done some work in connection with her studies at the Buenos Aires embassy of a country which accepts Argentinian political refugees: that could have been the reason for her detention.

It had been comparatively easy to check Josefina's case with the help of the vast documentation available to AI. Its comprehensive and painstaking research, since its beginnings in 1961, into political imprisonment, prison conditions, torture, legislation on human rights, trials, capital punishment, amnesties and so on, is the very core of AI's activities. Occasionally, it may be used as a research source by journalists and governments, historians and human rights organizations.

Research is only the first stage of AI's work; the information is quickly channelled into action. Josefina's case went to the coordination unit which selected an adoption group for her: a group in Northern France, to complete its essential, impartial balance of three adoptees — one in a left-wing, one in a right-wing, one in a non-aligned country. The group started at once campaigning for Josefina's release. Letters were sent to the Argentine Embassy in Paris, to the Minister of Justice in Buenos Aires, to professional bodies, to church organizations. On the advice of the International

Secretariat, the group also wrote to Josefina herself, hoping that the letter would reach her and give her comfort in her predicament, and to her family; some money was collected and sent to them by safe channels.

New information about the conditions of her imprisonment was reaching the International Secretariat. She had been sexually abused, beaten, and tortured with electric shocks despite her pregnancy. Now the Amnesty Campaign Against Torture also took up her case; more letters of protest and cabled requests for her release were sent to the Argentine authorities by many of the two thousand adoption groups which exist in three dozen countries. The international press reported on the case, briefed by AI supporters.

But Josefina was still in prison; seven months after her arrest, she gave birth to a boy. During labour, it was alleged, she was tied to a stretcher by her hands and feet until twenty minutes before delivery, and she was completely unattended until the last few minutes. The baby had to sleep on the floor of her rat-infested cell. The campaign for her release, the pressure on the Argentine authorities intensified. She had still not been charged. At last, thirteen months after her arrest, the news came: she had been freed from prison.

How Amnesty Works

The case of Josefina A., who had never been told why she was imprisoned at all, may seem typical, but there are no really typical cases. Each concerns a different human being, and each of them has to be helped in different ways according to circumstances. AI's long experience, its successes and disappointments over the years, serve as guidance when the most promising kinds of action are chosen. Usually, it is a combination of actions which may have the greatest effect; individual AI members and adoption groups have a handbook which tells them what to do, and gives them the rules to which everybody in the movement must adhere. This is essential for the movement as a whole, but not so easy to enforce — with a membership fast approaching the 200,000 mark all over the world and in countries with very different social and political backgrounds and traditions.

AI's monthly Newsletter keeps them all in constant touch with developments, and presents to them the cases of three 'Prisoners of the Month', selected by the Research Department of the International Secretariat: three prisoners of conscience who are in urgent need of help because they may be facing imminent execution, be in extreme ill-health, or have been detained in severe conditions for a long time. Again, these three critical cases are being selected to reflect the political impartiality of the movement.

An estimated 20,000 members can be expected to participate in each monthly campaign. Successes, as we know, cannot be claimed with any precision, but figures may give some guidance: in 1977-78, for instance, about 5,000 prisoners were under adoption or investigation by the groups; over 2,000 new prisoners were taken up (some of them by two or even three groups simultaneously) — and nearly 1,500 adopted prisoners were released.

What are the various actions which can be taken on behalf of urgent cases? There are, first of all, letters sent by members as individuals to the authorities concerned, appealing for the prisoners' release, the commutation of death sentences, etc. Such letters must be carefully phrased to avoid the impression of prejudice or aggressiveness. AI gives its members a number of samples while emphasizing that they are only meant to give some idea of possible approaches — it would obviously be wrong if thousands of letters were almost identical: this would destroy the spontaneity of the correspondence with the authorities. For instance, a letter (translated into the language of the addressee) about a prisoner of conscience to the Head of State and/or the Minister of Justice of the country concerned may be phrased like this:

'Your Excellency,

I am writing to you at this time to seek your assistance in establishing certain legal and personal details in the case of . . . ., a citizen of your country, at present believed to be detained under the Regulation for the Suppression of Rebellion. I am making enquiries into this case on behalf of Amnesty International, an independent non-governmental body in consultative status with the United Nations and UNESCO. It acts in defence of men and women who are imprisoned in violation of the Universal Declaration of Human Rights. In view of this mandate, AI would be failing in its duty if it did not make persistent efforts to investigate any case which might fall within its purview. It may interest you to know that the AI group to which I belong is currently working for the release of Mr./Mrs./ Miss . . . . . who has been held without trial for . . . years. I should be grateful if you would inform me of the details of the case.'

Or the letter may point out that the writer's country has extensive relations with that of the addressee, and that the AI group which has adopted the prisoner in question has been in touch with its own Department of Foreign Affairs:

'We gave information to the Department concerning Amnesty International's recent reports of serious violations of human rights in your country and requested that they take this serious situation into consideration in their relations with your country .... It is clear that the case of the prisoner X offers a disturbing example of serious infringements of the Universal Declaration of Human Rights, and we expressed our concern that toleration of these infringements by our government should not be allowed to continue. May I ask you to do everything in your power to investigate the conditions of detention of X. For your information, I have enclosed a brief description of his/her case. In particular, I am concerned about the welfare of his/her family who, I understand, are facing severe financial difficulties'.

Letters or postcards may also be written *en masse*: AI members can distribute the details of cases through kindred organizations or institutions, and to the general public with a request that all interested people write individually on behalf of the prisoners. Attempts may be made to secure the support of prominent citizens in the members' communities, asking them to participate in the campaign.

Members can prepare petitions on behalf of prisoners and circulate the petitions for signature among friends, professional colleagues, and other people interested in human rights. The local press is often asked to publish articles about prisoners' cases each month to create a wider protest; sympathetic institutions should be encouraged to write about them in their own publications. Once in a while, a local AI group — if there is one — may hold a public meeting to publicize critical cases and adopt resolutions. In some countries, concerts or bazaars are organized to collect money for prisoners' families. In London, big Amnesty variety performances with famous show personalities, who give their services free for the sake of AI's cause, have proved a magnificent way of raising funds and of keeping Amnesty's name in the public mind.

'Each case is an instance of acute personal suffering,' says the AI handbook for its members, 'of a human being detained unjustly, severed from normal life by the failure of governments to obey universal standards of decency and human rights. To illustrate this, each year AI selects a dozen cases of prisoners of conscience for special action during "Prisoner of Conscience Week" (the second week of October) — as symbols of the individual distress of all prisoners being adopted or investigated by AI members throughout the world.' During that week, members are asked to conduct special programmes to awaken popular understanding and stimulate protests. The media are usually cooperative in publicizing the cases of prisoners on the basis of material supplied by Amnesty groups or sections. Concerts, plays, public meetings and poster displays are organized to inform people about the work of AI, to raise funds and to recruit new members.

Sending greetings cards to prisoners is an important activity of members, for they remind detainees that they are not forgotten. Each year, in connection with Human Rights Day, December 10, the International Secretariat selects the cases of three dozen political prisoners for a special campaign of greetings cards in which all members are asked to take part. Even in cases where the cards do not reach the prisoner, the authorities concerned are reminded that their prisoners are not forgotten, and may be moved to acts of clemency. Often enough, there is no reply to the cards and letters, but members keep writing them for months and even years.

Frequently, AI sends distinguished international lawyers or leading defenders of human rights on missions to various countries and to conferences to represent the movement, conduct negotiations on its behalf — officially or, perhaps even more effective, unofficially — to collect on-the-spot information about prisoners of conscience or legal procedures. AI observers are sent to important or controversial trials, though they are often refused admission by dictatorial regimes. The reports of these missions are then, as a rule, submitted privately to the governments in question before they are published.

From the very beginning of AI's work, the adoption group has been the basic unit for action. But although groups exist in about three dozen countries, individual members and supporters are spread over more than a hundred countries. National sections for coordinating activities in their respective areas exist in well over thirty countries, including some which have themselves come under AI's fire such as Bangladesh, Ghana, Sri Lanka, South Korea, India, and Nigeria. A number of smaller countries, especially· Switzerland, Austria, Holland, and Denmark, have done very well with their relatively large number of adoption groups. On the other hand, the United States, a latecomer, was something of a disappointment, until recent years when it has grown in number of groups and support staff dramatically. France's national section, established in 1964, began to slacken after a few years, though some one hundred and fifty adoption groups survived and have gone on to become one of the fastest growing national sections in the organisation. A new coordinating committee was set up in Spain in 1977, and adoption groups began to form. Sweden has always been a strong Amnesty supporter; it has two hundred and fifty adoption groups.

The Italians, too, with Mussolini's dictatorship still in their minds, started one of the earliest national sections, yet the country's own precarious political and economic situation seems to have prevented its people from taking much interest in an international movement such as Amnesty. Western Germany, with over five hundred adoption groups, is extremely active; it has developed some original ways of helping Amnesty — such as asking mourners, by advertisement, to send no flowers to the funeral but gifts of money to AI instead. The German Federal post has issued Amnesty stamps.

One would expect the national section of Amnesty's birthplace and the seat of its headquarters, Britain, to be the comparatively largest, but it was quite small — with only two thousand members — until 1974. Then, however, the section decided to break with its characteristically English tradition of voluntary, unpaid work, and engaged a staff of full-time, salaried campaign workers under an energetic expert, David Simpson, as the section's new director. Within three years, membership figures more than trebled, reaching six thousand five hundred by 1978. Largely thanks to Simpson's efforts, Britain is now the country where the movement has the greatest influence on public opinion: every day Amnesty is mentioned in the media in some context and the press takes it for granted that readers are interested in the movement. Radio and television give it very good coverage, thereby confirming its status in the public mind. In one respect, however, the Irish section is one -up on the British: in Eire, four thousand schools receive AI's literature and posters for display.

The budget of the International Secretariat of AI has risen enormously; at the end of the 1970s, it surpassed one million pounds per year, contributed — in proportion to their size — by the national sections. A large part of it is being spent on publications — up to twenty, from briefing booklets to substantial volumes of reports on individual countries (plus over 70 news releases), are being printed each year, many in a number of languages. Apart from English, French and Spanish are the languages in which publications are in the greatest demand, but Slavonic and South Asian languages as well as Arabic, Dutch, Danish, Finnish, German, Greek, Icelandic, Italian, Japanese, Korean, and Swedish are scheduled to follow. Of course, many national sections have AI material translated and published in their own languages, but this puts a great burden on their financial resources, and the International Secretariat will relieve them of it wherever possible.

AI headquarters do not have a large staff. The work of the International Secretariat has been spread very thinly over a large area. If staff members are ill, on leave, or on a mission, they leave a gap that may cause delays and administrative confusion. Yet suitable people for a kind of work for which there is no specialized training elsewhere are hard to find — and every penny paid for salaries in London may have to come out of some quota for assistance to those who need it most. Fortunately, things have become a little easier since AI had a welcome windfall, quite out of the blue, in 1977; more about it later.

'Whatever is said . . . '

The very impartiality of Amnesty's work for human rights has provoked, almost inevitably, criticisms and attacks from all sides — right and left, from the media and from governments — and the more Amnesty grew into a real power all over the world, the louder became those voices of the defenders of injustice, perpetrated for political reasons. From the one side, the movement is accused of doing the Kremlin's dirty work, from the other, of being the imperialists' lackey — the best proof that it is truly independent and unbiassed. But the voices of those who have been helped by Amnesty and of those who praise it as an instrument of humanity and sanity are also making themselves heard, and among the hundreds of tributes there are two which the Amnesty people like to quote in the face of defamation.

One is by Leonid Plyushch, the Soviet mathematician detained for years in a psychiatric hospital, who was granted an exit visa in 1976 after a long campaign on his behalf by AI and other organizations:

> 'I would like to ask the press to convey my gratitude to all those who played a part in my release — to the International Committee of Mathematicians, to Amnesty International, to the workers' syndicates of France, to the Ukrainian organisations throughout the world, to the British, French and German psychiatrists, to the Committee against the Use of Psychiatry for Criminal Ends in the USSR . . . . '

The other quotation comes from an editorial in the *New York Post* in 1975 after the Governor of New York State had granted executive clemency to Martin Sostre, falsely convicted of selling heroin and sentenced to forty years' imprisonment. Many people felt that he had been framed because of his political activities on behalf of black Americans. The newspaper wrote:

'Governor Carey's decision to grant clemency to Martin Sostre is a victory for the conscience of mankind and, more specifically, for the dedicated efforts of every human being associated with Amnesty International'.

The Soviet regime, of course, expressed quite different opinions of Amnesty, particularly when Russian ways of treating political prisoners had been revealed. In 1971, *Izvestia* wrote: 'Especially zealous is the notorious Amnesty International, whose unscrupulous methods we have already related,' and went on to attack it because of its disclosures regarding dissenting intellectuals locked up in psychiatric hospitals: 'The western ideological saboteurs who babble all kinds of rubbish about mentally ill persons do not even notice what a ridiculous position they are putting themselves in.' Byelorussia's Party newspaper attacked AI in 1974 for 'defending anti-Communists' in the Soviet Union while 'doing nothing for the thousands of citizens languishing in Chilean, Spanish, Israeli and South African jails as these prisoners are not anti-Communists'. The *Pravda Ukrainy* in Kiev declared in 1970 that AI was, 'even according to the bourgeois press, in a leading position among organizations which conduct subversive anti-Soviet propaganda . . . AI disseminates falsified material in capitalist countries . . . . The philanthropists resort to cruel slander.'

In September, 1975, a glowing tribute to AI came over the air to short-wave listeners: 'Amnesty International has issued a revealing document. It confirms, with the authority of this humanitarian international organization, the violation of human rights, arbitrariness in the administration of justice, repression as a form of government . . . .' Where did these words come from? — Radio Moscow. But then, Amnesty's 'revealing document' was not dealing with Russia, but with Franco's Spain.

In 1978, David Simpson, director of the British section of AI, published a hard-hitting article about Russia's treatment of its dissidents in the London *Guardian*. A quick reaction from Moscow came by the Tass news agency, whose commentator, Yuri Kornilov, replied that wherever there were Soviet dissidents there were traces of western secret services — and that Amnesty International received regular subsidies from America's CIA.

Prague's *Tribuna* regarded (1975) AI as an organization specially created by 'imperialist centres', assisted by emigrés, for helping those sentenced for 'acts of subversion'. Already in 1966, the East German *Berliner Zeitung* wrote that it was 'absurd' of AI 'to focus on the GDR as there are no political prisoners in our country'. In a similar vein, Ghana's *Weekly Spectator* called AI (in 1972) 'this imperialist body', whose 'advice of a diabolic nature' on the treatment of Ghana's political detainees 'can only breed confusion and dissaffection and must therefore be rejected outright with deserving contempt'. A year later, Accra's *Daily Graphic* called AI 'a dangerous international political organization which pokes its dirty nose in the affairs of other countries'. When Amnesty sent a French lawyer to attend the trials of dissidents in Senegal, her President Senghor commented: 'I do not have particularly warm feelings for them (the AI observers). Quite often, I find that their positions are marked by racism, or at least paternalism. They protest rarely against the violence exercised in developed countries, and there are certain silences which are cowardly.'

Another African president, Idi Amin of Uganda, devoted one of his speeches at the UN General Assembly (in 1975) to AI which 'has blackmailed over one hundred nations of the world as violators of human rights without mentioning Britain and her role in Northern Ireland. AI is fed on rumours and concoctions from discredited criminals in exile . . . . They have lent themselves as tools for the smear campaigns perpetrated by the colonial and imperialistic powers that fund their existence.'

South Africa, of course, has a different official attitude to Amnesty, whose correspondence files contain a letter from Mr. Vorster's private secretary, answering a protest against the forced resettlement of black Africans in 1972. This it says, is 'typical of Amnesty International' which takes exception to that resettlement, while 'the murder of 80,000 black people in the Sudan and elsewhere is apparently condoned or shrugged off'. The letter suggests to AI that it should rather 'approach certain prominent member states of the Organization of African Unity and its friends behind the Iron Curtain'.

For the South American dictators, too, Amnesty is a tool of the Communists. 'Shaking with rage, Mr. Martinez (Argentina's Ambassador to the UN) dismissed evidence from Amnesty International that up to six thousand political prisoners are detained in Argentina as "absurd accusations",' a London paper reported from the Geneva UN conference on the protection of minorities in 1977. A journal in Buenos Aires claimed in 1975 that AI 'systematically accuses the governments of countries such as Brazil and Chile . . . while downplaying or completely omitting the undoubtedly far graver crimes against humanity that take place in the Communist-ruled states'.

125

O Cruzeiro in Rio de Janeiro called (in 1972) AI an 'instrument of Communist terrorism which, from London, aids guerillas throughout the world . . . by means of lies and defamations against democratic governments . . . . It has conducted a systematic campaign against Brazil, inventing tortures, assassinations and acts of violence in order to promote Communist objectives.' The Mexican *Replica* came, in 1975, to the aid of a neighbouring country: 'Amnesty International barks once again with slanders and lies, endeavouring to stain the honour and international prestige of that great Latin American nation, the heroic republic of Guatemala.' *La Mañana* in Montevideo published a cartoon which has become the movement's prize exhibit: the devil, labelled 'Amnesty International', bearing files with the headings 'Calumnies', 'Lies', and 'Defamation'.

Like the African 'Third World' countries, those in Asia were at first highly satisfied with AI's work — until they themselves had to be charged with imprisoning, killing, or torturing their opponents. An Iran journal called AI simply 'this espionage agency'. Even that cradle of Eastern wisdom, India, found itself in Amnesty's firing line when its then Prime Minister, Indira Gandhi, declared a state of emergency, suspended fundamental human rights, and detained tens of thousands of alleged opponents of her regime. AI and other international organizations urged their release, and Mrs. Gandhi said in an interview with the journal of her own party, *Socialist India*: 'We learn that the Socialist International and Amnesty International are two organizations which are very active in the hate-India campaign. They are flush with funds. One wonders where these come from.'

Arief Budiman, one of the most active and courageous student leaders in Indonesia, published, in 1973, an article in a leading news magazine which hit the nail on the head:

'If the Indonesian government is hostile to this organization (AI) and regards it as a Communist group, then this attitude will bolster the Communist groups which campaign for political purposes. In Europe everybody knows that Amnesty International is a non-political organization which is viewed with enmity by both the Spanish and Greek governments and the governments in Eastern Europe.'

Or, as George H. Nash put it in the New York *National Review* in 1974: 'After surveying the evidence, I do not believe that Amnesty practises a systematic double standard. To its enduring credit,

Amnesty's concern appears to be genuinely universal.' Another American writer, Martha Gelhorn, who was married to Ernest Hemingway, visited Spain after Franco's death and sent AI a note which the International Secretariat treasures in its files:

'In poor Basque villages even teenage boys spoke of Amnesty International (perhaps the only English word they knew), and a returned political prisoner explained how much it meant to them, in jail, to feel that this organization existed and they were not forgotten by the world. Where police torture is routine, as in Spain and most especially in the Basque country, Amnesty gives hope of being heard: Amnesty is the only place to send word of such official crimes and – in the simplest terms – Amnesty is seen as a friend by all those who suffer for expressing their opposition to the injustices and abuses of a police state.'

A few years ago, AI showed its traditional pluck (and sense of humour) by publishing a booklet of quotes from printed attacks by its detractors on the right and left all over the world. Its members accept, with a good grace, the fact that he who sticks his neck out must be prepared to get mud in his eye. The booklet had a motto of some verses by the seventeenth-century poet Jean de la Fontaine, the famous author of the *Fables*:

'It is impossible to please everybody and his father.
But whether I am blamed or praised,
Whatever is said or not said about me,
I shall go my own way.'

The Peace Prize – and After

On October 10, 1977, Amnesty International was awarded the Nobel Peace Prize, with a cheque for £80,000 to follow two months later in Oslo on December 10, which is the annual prize-giving date as well as Human Rights Day. The Luxembourg parliament had nominated the movement for the prize. As soon as AI heard the great news it held a press conference, making a plea to all governments for the release of prisoners of conscience and for the abolition of torture and the death penalty. At the same time, AI appealed to people everywhere to sign its Prisoners of Conscience Year petition, also addressed to all governments and the United Nations, demanding the release of non-violent prisoners and universal respect for human rights.

The citation of the Norwegian Nobel Peace Prize Committee said that AI had 'used its forces to protect the value of human life.

Amnesty International has given practical humanitarian and impartial support to people who have been imprisoned because of their race, religion or political views'. Messages of congratulation from governments, organizations and individuals, including former prisoners of conscience, poured into AI's London headquarters.

The British and the Irish press applauded wholeheartedly. 'Nobel Prize for diplomatic clout', the *Guardian* in London headed its tribute, which said: 'It takes much more, of course, than seemingly simple protests to dislodge monolithic repression and let even one victim crawl out from underneath it. It is here that Amnesty's diplomatic clout comes into action, and its unseen powers of persuasion do their work. There are "ambassadors" and missions putting the pressure on at that finely calculated point when a government might be embarrassed or shamed into action . . . . To avoid the embarrassment of accepting funds from governments or major corporations, Martin Ennals's (the Secretary General's) rule is that he holds up each pound note to the light.'

The *Economist*, also published in London, wrote in its congratulatory article: 'No doubt one could devise a more efficient watchdog. Since such a one does not exist, all thanks should be given to those do-gooders who, for no material return, snip and snipe at an unknown government on behalf of an unknown person. May they go on, doing just that.' The *Irish Times* told its readers: 'This organization is one of the many which we have praised when it suited us, ignored or recoiled from when it sought to do here what we had applauded when done elsewhere.' But some other Irish comments pointed out that the award was almost a duplication — Sean MacBride had received the Nobel Peace Prize only three years earlier, also for his defence of human rights. The *Indian Express* said: 'The Nobel Committee has widened the area of selection to include a field despised by many established governments.' A Dutch paper headed its news item: 'Scolded from Left and Right'. A French journal suggested, 'You can send Amnesty flowers, nice words, or pennies. But you can also become an active member and start a group!'

It was to be expected that the Peace Prize would be resented as an affront in those countries which had been attacked by AI because of their violations of human rights; as usual, it was charged with political bias. One South American voice, however, added praise to its condemnation: 'The Prize was awarded to Amnesty which on many occasions played along with international Marxism by only attacking anti-Marxist countries,' said Radio Agricultura in Santiago, Chile. 'But now that attitude has changed, and AI has begun to defy the wrath of the Communists by denouncing violations of human rights in Moscow itself.' Reuter reported from Montevideo: 'Uruguayan Foreign Minister Sr. Rovira accused AI of acting very deviously and falsely in the case of Uruguay. "What has never been established," he added, "is Amnesty's impartiality.".' The Uruguayan Minister of Education called the award 'a joke in bad taste'. In Jakarta, the Chief of Indonesia's security forces, Admiral Sudomo, used the occasion of the Nobel award again to protest against AI's claim that his country had 100,000 political prisoners. 'This is a blatant lie,' he declared. 'There are no more than 31,500. That organization should change its name to "Amnesty Communist International"!'

There was no unfriendly comment on the award from the eastern bloc − simply because there was no word about the Prize at all, except for a snide remark in Moscow's international shortwave service: that it was just 'an episode in the vast campaign conducted by certain western circles'. As though by higher command, the media in most Communist countries kept completely silent; even at the Belgrade conference which began in the same week when the award was announced − the follow-up meeting of the 1975 Helsinki Agreement countries − the very name Amnesty was avoided by the eastern delegates like hell-fire. One Russian, however, commented in his own way: Valentin Turchin, the former chairman of the Moscow AI adoption group, left for his enforced exile in the United States that week. Only the Yugoslav spokesman in Belgrade, at his press briefing, replied to the journalists' questions on what he thought of the award: he was 'surprised', he said. Of course, Yugoslavia had also been a few times in AI's line of fire, particularly after the Croat students' riots of 1971 when hundreds were arrested.

Strangely enough, the German Federal Republic was the only West European country where Amnesty's award met with some bilious remarks. 'The practices of the bestowers remain mysterious,' wrote the conservative *Münchner Merkur*, while the influential *Frankfurter Allgemeine Zeitung* declared: 'This organization has, for the most part, seen political persecution and torture only in the western world. It has mostly left out the eastern bloc.' The writer was inadequately informed: AI had just published its latest briefing paper on human rights violations in the other Germany, the GDR, with estimates of several thousand political prisoners serving sentences of up to three years for trying to leave the country; the report attacked the continued practice of prolonged pre-trial detention, the imprisonment of citizens who criticize official policy, and the severe restrictions on freedom of movement, expression and association.

No argument for Amnesty's continued indispensability was needed, yet South Africa provided it only a few days after the Nobel award. One morning at four o'clock the telephone rang at the bedside of the Rev. Paul Oestreicher, Vicar of the Church of Ascension in the London suburb of Blackheath and Chairman of the British Amnesty section. A woman's voice said, 'The security branch are in the next room. They are taking everything away. We have been banned, and so have eighteen other organizations. Tell the world.' Then the line went dead.

This was how the news of the Pretoria government's biggest clamp-down on black movements first reached the western world. James Kruger, the South African Minister of Justice, had not only banned those movements — among them 'Black Consciousness' and the Christian Institute — but also two newspapers. Many offices and homes were raided and at least fifty people arrested. Kruger defended his action as 'necessary for the maintenance of law and order', authorised under the 1976 Internal Security Act, previously called the Suppression of Communism Act. When the name was changed, new clauses were added empowering the authorities to ban organizations and arrest individuals not suspected of being Communist, but simply deemed to be a threat to the South African establishment.

'This time it really looks as though the lights are going out in South Africa,' commented a London paper. 'It is a suicidal course.'

AI's explanation for the timing of the unprecedented action by the Vorster regime was that it wanted to silence all criticism of the security forces for their handling of the Steve Biko affair. An Amnesty cable had been sent to Kruger urging an open and independent inquiry into the death of the thirty-year-old leader of the Black Consciousness movement who was reported to have died while in security police custody. It was the twentieth death in detention of a political prisoner within eighteen months. 'It is widely believed,' commented AI, 'that several detainees at least have been tortured to death during interrogation by security police who then faked the circumstances to give the appearance of suicide.' There was a long drawn-out inquest on Biko's death. The post-mortem spoke of extensive brain injury, kidney failure, uraemia. Witnesses said that he had been kept naked, in leg-irons and manacles on the floor of his cell; that he had been transported, still naked and chained, in a Land-Rover on a one thousand two hundred kilo-metre, fourteen-hour journey from the prison in Port Elizabeth to Pretoria. There he died the next night. No charges were made against the police.

When, a few months later, a United States representative called upon the UN Human Rights Commission to reopen investigations into Biko's death, he explained his country's reason for its interest in the case: 'Biko was a man of giant moral stature who held out the promise of saving South Africa from self-destruction.'

6

Human Rights and Power Politics

The Report that was Leaked

The Amnesty movement has often been accused, by critics in foreign countries, of being a tool of the British government. These voices were abruptly silenced in June, 1978, when a full-scale row broke out over an AI report on the maltreatment of suspected terrorists in Northern Ireland by the Royal Ulster Constabulary. By implication, it accused the British authorities of condoning brutal and humiliating methods of interrogation. It was the third time in seven years that Amnesty had launched a massive indictment of these authorities.

Half of the 70-page report consisted of an examination of 78 separate allegations of physical and mental ill-treatment; in 30 of these cases, an Amnesty team heard evidence from doctors — but not from police doctors, for the Northern Ireland authorities refused to make their files available to Amnesty. The report, however, makes the point that no uniformed policemen were involved in the allegations, only RUC detectives; another important point was that among the victims were both Republican and Loyalist suspects.

The detectives, alleged the report, were using 'psychologically exhausting procedures' during interrogations, the humiliation and derision of prisoners. Some were threatened with death, a woman with rape; one prisoner said that the interrogators had ridiculed his genitals. It was 'standard practice' to deny the access to solicitors to people arrested under the provisions of emergency legislation.

The list of physical maltreatment methods reads hardly different from allegations against the police in countries less bound by the rule of law than Britain. Suspects had been made to stand or sit on the floor during lengthy periods of questioning; they were choked, hooded, deprived of sleep, their wrists were twisted, their skin burnt with cigarettes. Witnesses claimed that they had been struck in the face and stomach, kicked on the legs and buttocks, beaten on the head; one prisoner alleged that his head was banged against a wall and that he had been lifted up by his ears, another said that soiled underpants were put over his face. Prisoners complained that they had, after interrogation, 'a recurrent feeling of walking upside down'.

The Amnesty team, which had worked in Ulster in the winter of 1977/78, consisted of two Danish doctors, a Dutch lawyer, and an AI researcher. Before publication, the report — which called for a 'public and impartial' inquiry into the allegations — was submitted to the British government and especially to the Northern Ireland Secretary; the only other copies then in existence were locked in AI's International Secretariat. But suddenly, the press and other media in the United Kingdom and in the Irish Republic began to write about, and discuss, the still unpublished report, quoting extensive details of the investigators' findings. Who had 'leaked' the report? The source was traced to Dublin, but it could only have been the British government from where the information had come.

What could it had tried to achieve by that leak? The most plausible explanation was that the British authorities had hoped to 'defuse' Amnesty's allegations so that the media would drop the report, when it was officially published, in the waste-paper basket as old hat. The device did not work; hurriedly, the AI Executive Committee decided to publish at once, ten days earlier than originally intended. Surprisingly, the media picked it up again and discussed it at great length. The leak had, in fact, proved counterproductive. An inquiry into the allegations had to be started; however, it was an internal government affair, neither public nor independent, and interminable like most official inquiries.

There was another behind-the-scenes action which did not work either. The Northern Ireland Secretary was said to have been 'leaning' on the British Independent Television Authority to ban a documentary programme on Amnesty's report. When the television station concerned decided to replace it by a comedy show, the technicians refused to transmit it — and for half an hour the viewers' screens remained blank. But the BBC got hold of the banned programme and transmitted it before the Secretary or any other government office knew about that 'switch' and had time to try and suppress it. As a result, Amnesty's report received more coverage in the British media than any other AI publication had had for years!

Not all the reaction, however, was sympathetic to Amnesty's concern about the treatment of suspects in Ulster. 'Like other terrorist organisations', said a typical reader's letter to a London paper, 'the IRA demands impeccable standards of fairness and moral rectitude from the countries and organisations they attack, while they themselves feel free to subject individuals to sadistic and inhuman cruelty. As long as such gross double standards exist, the public reaction to Amnesty's no doubt reasonably accurate report will be: so what?' There was also a record volume of 'hate mail' on AI's desks — including letters asking indignantly why the movement had decided to publish its report without discussing it first with the British government. . . . . !

'Don't Cry for me, Argentina'

It was to be expected that AI would do its utmost to remind soccer fans everywhere that the 1978 World Cup matches would take place in a country where, during the preceding two years of military rule, fifteen thousand people had been murdered, jailed, tortured, or abducted without trace. Argentina's regime could not be allowed to get away with the prestige boost it was hoping for when millions of people all over the world would be watching the great event. Already two months before its beginnings, Amnesty's West German section spoke to the country's Soccer Association about pointing out Argentina's violations of human rights to soccer fans 'without spoiling their enjoyment of the sport'. The outcome of the talks was a national campaign under the motto: 'Soccer, yes — Torture, no'.

A former soccer international, Derek Dougan, was to cover the World Cup for British television. Before he went, he wrote a leading article for Amnesty's journal. ' "Don't cry for me, Argentina", runs a popular song,' he said. 'The world should cry out loud for Argentina's prisoners of conscience . . . The very football grounds [football is what the British call soccer] where we shall see the matches played have been the scenes of their persecution. The World Cup will be a shop window for the military authorities, anxious to cast a pleasant image to the world. Football is one thing; thousands of prisoners of conscience another. The World Cup should not distract our attention from what remains when the final has been played.'

Was AI's World Cup campaign a success? It is difficult to say, and Amnesty's headquarters showed their usual reluctance to claim any positive results such as prisoners' release. Although the soccer reporters were anxious not to spoil their readers' 'enjoyment of the sport' by writing about political persecution, a good many newspapers in various countries mentioned Argentina's brutal record in matters of human rights in their editorial columns.

The Argentinian government of General Jorge Rafael Videla seemed to be little impressed by these international criticisms of its methods; it relied on the sports enthusiasts' aversion to having their fun spoiled by such irrelevancies as human rights. To make sure that politics were kept out of the picture the government had hired one of the most expensive U.S. public relations agencies to 'raise a sweet-smelling and pastel-coloured smokescreen', as a British journalist called it, in front of the brutal reality of Argentina's dictatorship. And in order to avoid the visitors' contacts with critics of the regime, about fifty Argentinian journalists, professional people and other 'unreliable' intellectuals were abducted by the security forces during the matches. They disappeared without trace, according to an exiled leading member of the Argentine Commission for Human Rights.

A particularly ghastly story from that unhappy country was told to AI in London in the autumn of 1978 by one of those dozens of South American refugees who seek help abroad in tracing their relatives who have disappeared. Laura Bruchstein, a Jewish woman from Buenos Aires, had lost her husband and two of her four children – dead or missing after having been taken away by the security forces. One day she received a terrible gift: a jar with two severed hands – those of her eldest daughter. The army authorities brought them to her; they had been cut off for 'identification', she was told, after the 24-year old girl and her husband had been captured, executed as guerillas, and buried in a mass grave south of Buenos Aires. The horrified mother sued the army for murder. Soon afterwards, Laura Bruchstein's husband, a chemist, was arrested; she never saw him again. But a nurse who had tended him in a hospital told her that an officer shouted at him: 'How dare a Jewish bastard sue the Argentine army!' In 1977, the youngest daughter and her husband were also abducted by a military patrol; their two babies were left lying on the pavement.

Amnesty was equally concerned about other Latin American countries. It released details of 113 death-squad killings and abductions in Guatemala during the last quarter of 1977, each case symptomatic of a 'long-standing pattern of political murder and intimidation'. Since 1966, twenty thousand Guatemalans out of a population of four million had died in the hands of paramilitary groups 'whose actions are characterized by a total immunity before the law'.

'Deaths under Torture in Uruguay' was the title of an AI report published in May, 1978. It described in detail the cases of twelve people who had died in that country under torture during the preceding two years – a follow-up of Amnesty's earlier report on 22 Uruguayans who had died in custody between 1972 and 1975. Since then, claimed the new report, 'the use of torture had not diminished', and 2500 political prisoners were still believed to be held in Uruguay: one in every 1000 of the country's total population.

Reports from the Third World

In Africa, Ghana had gone through a long period of unrest under its ruler, General Acheampong – who was toppled by another General, Akuffo, in a 'palace coup' in July, 1978. He released most of the 300 members of the three opposition parties who had been detained when Acheampong declared his one-party state after a fake referendum, and there was some hope of a better future for Ghana.

But conditions in Guinea (Conakry), according to an AI report of 1978, were still appallingly bad. Under its ultra-left ruler since 1958, Ahmed Sekou Toure, who had been a promising poet in his young years, this little West African republic with its five million inhabitants was holding between 2000 and 4000 political prisoners in two main camps under extremely harsh conditions: 'They are completely isolated from the outside world and are not allowed to receive visits or even letters from their families. Many prisoners have been detained without trial for seven years; others were sentenced to life imprisonment after arbitrary legal proceedings at which they were not allowed to be present. . . . Torture has become an essential part of the machinery of repression . . . including the use of electric shocks, severe beatings, burning with cigarettes, and immersing head first in barrels of water. . . . Fingernails have been ripped out.'

Cautiously as usual, AI recorded some improvements since its report had been published, without claiming them as successes. A number of long-term political prisoners, including the Roman-Catholic Archbishop Tchidimbo, were said to have been released as Guinea was growing 'increasingly sensitive to international criticism on human rights issues'. But Amnesty explained that its normal technique of naming specific prisoners could not be used – to do so would condemn them to death because Sekou Toure might immediately order their execution. He had refused AI requests for permission to send observers to the prison camps. What had emerged from witnesses' reports was that there was no provision for doctors or even medical orderlies, that prisoners were allowed to wash only once in three weeks, that most of them were suffering from malaria, dysentry, scurvy, or beri-beri, and that many had been starved to death.

Kenya's President Jomo Kenyatta, who died in 1978, was widely respected as a wise and humane ruler; yet his country was by no means free of infringements of human rights. One of Amnesty's adopted prisoners, a left-wing professor of literature at Nairobi University and an internationally known author, Ngugi wa Thiong'o, was arrested and detained under the Preservation of Public Security Act in December, 1977. This Act allows people to be held indefinitely without trial or the opportunity to submit a legal defence as the charges were not stated. Amnesty could only guess why the professor was being kept behind bars, without visits, correspondence, writing materials and books: he had recently expressed his views on inequality and corruption in Kenya in a Kikuyu-language play (whose performance licence was suddenly withdrawn) and in his latest novel, *Petals of Blood*, widely read throughout Africa.

AI submitted its new report on Pakistan, drafted by a mission which had visited the country early in 1978, to its military government. But no comments came, and when news arrived that 140 journalists and editors had been arrested under a new martial law for criticising the government, the report was published. Some of these prisoners, after being sentenced by summary military courts, had been flogged; newspapers were closed down, presses confiscated. Well-known politicians, including the former Prime Minister Bhutto, were sentenced to death; some public executions took place in Lahore.

Amnesty's report expressed great concern at the practice of trying civilians, particularly political prisoners, before military courts, which do not allow for appeals to a higher court. AI demanded that the Pakistani government should immediately abolish flogging and that the death centences should be commuted; it also called for international observers to be admitted to political trials. The request to visit Mr. Bhutto in prison was refused. 'It is impossible to say, on the basis of the transcript supplied, whether Mr.

137

Bhutto's trial for ordering a political murder has been doctored,' stated AI in the report. Since its publication, several thousand more people were said to have been arrested.

Crackdown on the Dissidents
In the autobiographical novel *Ward* 7 by the exiled Soviet author Valery Tarsis there is a dialogue between the hero, a writer detained in a psychiatric hospital because he had his books published in the Western world, and a doctor who accuses him of spreading anti-Soviet propaganda abroad. The writer answers; 'The Soviet government itself has done this so effectively during the past half-century that I wouldn't dream of entering into competition with it!'

A good many people in the West will have thought on the same lines during the greater part of 1978 when the reports of the dissidents' trials dominated the media; those who were old enough to remember Stalin's 'Great Purge' of the 1930s were reminded of the show trials of alleged Trotskyites, which cost the Soviet Union masses of friends in the democratic countries. The new wave of dissidents' trials was even more harmful to the prestige of the Soviet Union, for it alienated even the Communist parties in the West. The leadership of the French party protested to Moscow, demanding 'an end to all prosecutions and repressions'; the Italian party leader, Beringuer, condemned the trials with the full backing of his executive; the British Communist Party issued a statement calling on the Soviet Union to rescind the sentences; Lars Werner, the Swedish Party chairman, spoke in a similar vein. No less significant was the start of an international campaign, supported by prominent, traditionally non-political sportsmen, to boycott the 1980 Olympic Games in Moscow.

Had the Soviet government expected these reactions, or had it miscalculated the outside world's sensitivity about human rights? Was this crackdown on the dissidents merely dictated by the Russian leaders' annoyance and nervousness about the growing internal criticism of the Soviet regime? Or did the men in the Kremlin feel so sure of Soviet power that they decided to risk the consequences, the damage to Russia's reputation and to foreign relations? Russian governments had always shown much disregard for outside reactions, not only during the 1930s but right back in tsarist times. But perhaps the new trials were just a clumsy attempt at silencing the dissident movement in good time for the Olympic Games with their inevitable influx of nosy foreigners. If so, that action had exactly the opposite effect — as many actions of Russia's leaders had had before: their understanding of non-Russian mentality had always been rather poor.

What must have surprised them more than any other forms of protest, however, was the sudden elevation of the whole issue into the lofty sphere of power politics. U.S. President Carter made the trials his personal concern, maybe because of his own sincere feelings about human rights, perhaps in response to public or political pressure — or even, as some sceptics suspected, to bolster up his flagging popularity: whatever the reason, America and the Soviet Union found their relations sinking to the lowest ebb since the beginning of the Cold War; as a result, the world at large was facing a dangerous hardening of attitudes between the two super-powers.

This was particularly evident in Geneva, where a new round of talks on the limitation of strategic arms had started. Some hawks in Washington demanded the immediate suspension of the talks unless the Soviets stopped the trials. President Carter, it was disclosed, had tried to win freedom for the most endangered prisoners who were facing trial by way of an exchange deal, a swap of detainees as it had been arranged before, but this time Moscow wouldn't play.

Amnesty International might have been gratified that the great cause of human rights was now in the public eye as never before, but in fact the movement was somewhat embarrassed. To be sure, political prisoners are its concern, but political motives for human rights campaigns are a hindrance rather than a help. This world-wide yet one-sided American-led attack on a single offending country was threatening to overshadow Amnesty's campaigns against all the other violators of human rights.

Still, the prisoners in the Soviet docks had been adopted by AI and had to be supported by all means not only for humane reasons but because they represented, as David Simpson wrote in a London daily, 'a reliable human rights movement, nonpolitical, certainly not power-seeking, and strictly mandated to expose and try to correct human rights violations'. They were not really, he argued, 'dissidents' — a term implying general anti-Soviet opposition — but 'dissenters'; their dissent was 'from their government's claim that human rights violations do not occur in the USSR'. Yet the truth was that the Soviet government was acting against these monitors of the Helsinki Agreement in glaring contrast to that very agreement, whose 'Basket Three' said, essentially, that citizens of the signatory countries should be allowed freely to associate and to express their opinions, and that there should be 'room for an opposition' in every country.

That contrast emerged clearly enough at the trial in May, 1978 against the physicist Yuri Orlov, the founder of the monitoring groups. He had made himself the spokesman for many Soviet citizens who were asking whether their government had abided by the Helsinki stipulations; their complaints were circulated by *samizdat* bulletins, copies of which Orlov always sent to the authorities concerned. Among the reported abuses of human rights provisions were these: Prisoners had been made to suffer from hunger, cold, and lack of sleep; sick prisoners had been forced to work and were deprived of medical help; released prisoners had been banned from living with their families; sane prisoners had been confined in psychiatric hospitals, often together with violent patients, and were treated with harmful drugs; Jews had been refused permission to emigrate for unstated reasons, and many such *refusniki* — a sad new term in the Russian language — had been dismissed from their jobs, thus being reduced to poverty; Christian believers had been persecuted for practising their religion but were also denied permission to emigrate; Crimean Tartars, deported to Central Asia during the Second World War, who kept demanding their return, had their homes bulldozed and had been denied work.

These *samizdat* indictments were Orlov's real 'crime', but the charges against him were thinly veiled by spurious accusations that he had slandered the Soviet Union, and received money from Western agencies for publishing documents designed to 'undermine the foundations of the Soviet'. He had been in prison already for fifteen months when his trial began.

Dr. Andrei Sakharov, the most prominent critic of the regime still at liberty, was refused admission to the courtroom in Moscow; so were observers from the U.S. Embassy as well as Western journalists. AI observers did not get visas for the USSR to attend the trial. Orlov's wife was allowed to attend and was held standing as the sentence was read before an audience of obviously handpicked 'representatives of the public', who applauded and shouted: 'He deserves more!' That sentence was the maximum penalty laid down by Soviet law for offences against Article 70 of the Criminal Code — 'the systematic distribution of slanderous concoctions, smearing the Soviet state and social order with the object of weakening Soviet power': seven years in hard-labour camp and five more in internal exile, meaning Siberia.

There was a scuffle outside the courthouse at the end of the trial. Three hundred sympathizers with Orlov had assembled; Dr. Sakharov, who tried to force his way through, and half a dozen other dissidents were bundled into police vans. Western journalists who wanted to escort Orlov's wife to a safe place were filmed by KGB men.

Two months later the trials began against seven more dissidents, all of them AI's adopted prisoners of conscience. The two most prominent of them, both Jews, were Alexander Ginsburg, also a founding member of the Helsinki monitoring groups and the administrator of a relief fund for political prisoners and their families, who — though already a sick man — was sentenced to eight years' imprisonment; and Anatoly Shcharansky, who had already spent 14 months in detention and was sentenced to 13 years' imprisonment for 'treason in the form of espionage'. Ginsburg and his monitoring group were called 'hoodlums and bandits' by a prosecution witness; another witness testified that Ginsburg's children had 'bad morals' because they were listening to Voice of America broadcasts. At the Shcharansky trial, a court briefing was distributed to reporters claiming that the prisoner had contacts with 'an agent of the U.S. military intelligence', namely the Moscow correspondent of the *Los Angeles Times*: therefore, Shcharansky himself was a spy.

At Vilnius (Wilno) in Lithuania, the Roman-Catholic activist Viktoras Pyatkus, who ran the regional monitoring group, was sentenced to 15 years' imprisonment for 'anti-Soviet agitation and propaganda'; the same sentence, under the same charge, was handed to Levko Lukyanenko, a member of the Ukrainian monitoring group, at Kiev. The electronic engineer Vladimir Slepak, a Jewish friend of Orlov, who had attempted to get into the courtroom during Orlov's trial, was promptly arrested and sentenced to five years' exile for 'malicious hooliganism' — but his real offence was that he had displayed a placard demanding exit visas for his family from the balcony of his Moscow flat.

AI drew its supporters' special attention to the case of Alexander Podrabinek, a 25-year old medical assistant who had made an intensive study of the abuse of psychiatry by enforced treatment of dissenters in mental hospitals. The 265-page dossier he had compiled was smuggled to the West; an extensive summary was published by AI under the title *Punitive Medicine*. His trial was the last of the mid-1978 series. Podrabinek dismissed the Soviet lawyer assigned to him as his defence counsel and asked for the

London barrister Louis Blom-Cooper to be admitted instead. The barrister's request for a visa was refused; but he sent the court a file with the evidence of 15 witnesses who had testified to Podrabinek's honesty, scholarship and reliability.

Podrabinek's sentence was comparatively light: five years' internal exile. One of the reasons may have been that AI's extract with its case histories of over 200 detainees had played a major part at the World Psychiatric Conference at Honolulu in 1977, where it was accepted as evidence for Soviet methods. After the trial, a leading Moscow psychiatrist, Dr. Voloshanovich spoke out as one of the few Russian specialists to risk the consequences of challenging the Soviet authorities on the subject. He declared that he had examined 27 people listed by Podrabinek as political prisoners committed to psychiatric hospitals. 'Among those I examined,' said Dr. Voloshanovich, 'I found not a single case of definite mental illness . . . the Soviet psychiatrists who acquiesced in abuses of their profession were like doctors in Nazi Germany who tried to evade responsibility for war crimes by claiming they had acted only under orders.'

In some of the dissidents' trials, the prosecution added homosexuality to the usual list of political charges. Homosexuality is still a criminal offence in most Communist countries including the Soviet Union and certain Asian countries, and at AI's annual Council meeting in 1978 the Dutch delegates proposed that people imprisoned because of homosexual relations between consenting adults should be eligible for adoption as prisoners of conscience: were they not also covered by the concept of human rights?

The Dutch motion, supported by the U.S. delegates, caused a heated debate at the AI conference. The British and the Australian delegates argued that if it was accepted, this might lead to campaigns in aid of pederasts, exhibitionists, or even prostitutes as well. The term 'prisoners of conscience' would then lose much of its meaning. The Dutch proposal was rejected, but the British delegates stressed that the movement was certainly not unsympathetic to the human rights of persecuted homosexuals.

A New Kind of Trades Union

In a press statement in August, 1978, AI reported that it knew of more than 230 Soviet citizens who had been imprisoned, confined to mental hospitals, or exiled and deprived of their citizenship for non-violent exercise of their human rights during the preceding three years, since the Soviet government had signed the Helsinki

Agreement. Had it now smashed or at least silenced the human rights movement among its people? Oddly enough, its alternative policy of letting some critics of the regime go abroad or throwing them out continued simultaneously with the trials. Among them were the musicians Rostropovich and Vishnyevskaya, the painter Oscar Rabin — and the greatest troublemaker of them all, the former General Pyotr Grigorenko, now 70 years old. He was allowed to visit the United States together with his wife and stepson for a prostate operation. He had gone for a few weeks when Dr. Sakharov telephoned Western correspondents in Moscow that he had seen a decree, published in the official bulletin of the Supreme Soviet, stripping the war hero Grigorenko of his citizenship for his 'behaviour damaging to the prestige of the Soviet Union'. There was no other way for him but to ask for political asylum in the U.S. Sadly, he said: 'The Soviet Union is my fatherland, my life. It is my right to live in my fatherland, and I believe this will be so again one day.'

The unpredictability and arbitrariness of the Moscow leaders became evident already in 1972 when AI heard of the sentence passed in Kiev against Dr. Semyon Gluzman, a Soviet psychiatrist — seven years' jail and three years' exile in Siberia — for having diagnosed Grigorenko as mentally healthy when he was being kept in a mental hospital. The Swiss Amnesty branch launched an appeal for Dr. Gluzman's release.

Early in 1978, the British Amnesty section received some extraordinary Russian documents that had found their way to the West. There was a 46-year old miner who was being held in a Donetsk prison for having founded and organized a new kind of trades union. That man, Vladimir Klebanov, had spent twenty years in prisons, mental hospitals, and trying to find work.

His persecutions began when he attempted to persuade the official mineworkers' union, to which he belonged, to protest against the pit management's violations of health and safety regulations, and to demand 'correct' wages. That was in 1958, and ever since he had to fight desperately for his freedom and civil rights, for compensation and permission to work again. He failed all along the line; but he met fellow-workers who had suffered similar conditions in other industries. With some of them he founded the 'Association of Free Trades Unions'.

It was the first attempt since the 1917 revolution at creating a workers' union independent of the Soviet government. The next thing that happened was that Klebanov was arrested again, this

143

time charged with trying to blow up the Moscow Metro. But his Association spread and grew; at the time when Amnesty received the material there were already 200 supporters. One of the documents smuggled to London was a statement, signed by ten of them, that they had been detained for shorter or longer periods, four in psychiatric hospitals. The new trade union seemed to be gaining some influence, in fact so much that it could achieve Klebanov's release in January, 1978 — but after a few weeks the KGB got hold of him again, and he was sent to yet another mental clinic and then to prison. Obviously, the authorities were now preparing to put him on trial; but they must have been bewildered by the new situation: these dissidents were not intellectuals or professional people but, for the first time, simple workers protesting their treatment in a so-called workers' state!

The documents on the Association of Free Trades Unions were forwarded by Amnesty to the International Labour Organization (ILO); the Association also sent a plea for recognition to Britain's Trades Union Congress. Yet the TUC was reluctant. 'There is nothing we can do for these dissidents,' said the leader of one of the biggest British unions. 'We don't want to bugger up the close contacts we have built up with the official Russian unions. Of course, Russia is not a free country and we hate to turn down a body like Amnesty, but a lot of our executive members are looking forward to going on fraternal delegations to Moscow, and good luck to them.' AI was disappointed but not discouraged. It urged its own members to start a campaign for the imprisoned Soviet trade-unionists and their courageous leader Klebanov.

Today, such an Amnesty campaign is bound to make some impact on a government offending against human rights. The number of members is increasing with greater speed than ever before; at the time of writing it was a quarter of a million in 111 countries. Yet also rising seems to be the number of prisoners of conscience all over the world — or is it just that, thanks to Amnesty International, we hear more and are better informed about them than in previous years? The movement believes that an estimated half a million human beings who have committed no other crime than that of disagreeing with their governments are being deprived of their freedom: half a million flames of life flickering behind bars and barbed wire. But wherever there is some violation of human rights, people expect to hear from Amnesty about it.

* * *

'Open your newspaper any day of the week, and you will find a report from somewhere in the world of someone being imprisoned, tortured or executed because his opinions or religious beliefs are unacceptable to his government,' wrote Peter Benenson — the words with which he launched the Amnesty movement. They are, alas, as true today as they were in 1961. You may read that six hundred writers are imprisoned or persecuted in fifty-five countries, nearly a hundred doctors in twenty-five countries: all for political or religious reasons, or merely because they believe in the ethics of their professions. Muslim students are shot dead or arrested during peaceful demonstrations in Iran, Christians in Uganda, alleged revolutionaries in Morocco, alleged anti-revolutionaries in Ethiopia, trade-unionists in Peru and Chile. Thirty political prisoners are still confined to mental hospitals in Romania. A renowned Indonesian poet is arrested in Jakarta for 'exciting anti-government feelings' by reading his verses in public, a family of four in East Berlin for wanting to cross over to the West. In the USA, a black minister of the United Church of Christ, arrested after a civil rights demonstration, is still in gaol, sentenced to 'up to 34 years' imprisonment'; a Protestent pastor from Peking, arrested as a 'rightist' in 1957, is serving a life sentence. In South Africa, a dozen student leaders are on trial for their lives on charges arising from the Soweto riots in which well over five hundred blacks were killed by the security forces. . . . .

You may smile when you read that a South Korean university lecturer got into trouble for publishing a humorous story about a farmyard full of frightened chickens guarded by fierce watchdogs. The writer did not smile, for he was arrested when it dawned on the authorities that it was an allegory — the chickens were the South Koreans, the watchdogs President Park's KCIA.

You may despair at man's inhumanity to man. Is there nothing you can do to help, no weapon to defend your fellow-beings' rights, liberties, and lives? To fight the paranoic despots, the corrupt judges, the sadistic gaolers? You feel that, as an individual, you are helpless against the powers of evil. Is there not any league of men and women who are trying at least to do something about it?

Oh yes, there is.

Acknowledgments

The author and publishers are most grateful for the help given with information, archives material and illustrations for this book by those connected with Amnesty International and its staff, particularly by Peter Benenson; David Simpson, Director of the British Section; the Rev. Paul Oestreicher, Chairman of the British Section; Martin Enthoven, Head of Co-ordination Unit, Fran Taylor, Press Officer, Friederika Knabe, Head of Documentation Centre, John Humphreys, Head of Research, and Brian Wrobel, Death Penalty Conference Organizer, all of the International Secretariat. Thanks are also due to Diana Redhouse and the Amnesty staff Alison, Louise, Sasha, Sue, and Veronika for their valuable assistance.

147

Index